From Mounds to Mammoths

From Mounds

to Mammoths

A Field Guide to Oklahoma Prehistory

SECOND EDITION

Claudette Marie Gilbert
AND
Robert L. Brooks

University of Oklahoma
Press : Norman

LIBRARY OF CONGRESS CATALOGING-IN-PUBLICATION DATA
Gilbert, Claudette Marie.
From mounds to mammoths : a field guide to Oklahoma prehistory.—
2nd ed. / Claudette Marie Gilbert and Robert L. Brooks.
p. cm.
Rev. ed. of: Oklahoma prehistory / by Claudette Marie Gilbert. 1980.
Includes bibliographical references and index.
ISBN 0-8061-3225-6 (alk. paper)
1. Indians of North America—Oklahoma—Antiquities.
2. Indians of North America–Oklahoma–History.
3. Excavations (Archaeology)—Oklahoma.
4. Oklahoma—Antiquities.
I. Brooks, Robert L.
II. Gilbert, Claudette Marie.
Oklahoma prehistory.
III. Title.
E78.O45 .G54 2000 99-058190
976.6′01—dc21 CIP

Text design by Gail Carter.

The paper in this book meets
the guidelines for permanence
and durability of the Committee on
Production Guidelines for Book Longevity
of the Council on Library Resources, Inc.

2 3 4 5 6 7 8 9 10

Contents

Preface

Claudette Marie Gilbert wrote the first edition of *Oklahoma Prehistory* in 1980. The Oklahoma Archeological Survey and what is now called the Sam Noble Oklahoma Museum of Natural History published the volume through University Printing Services. By the early 1990s all twenty-five hundred copies of this document had been distributed to schools or sold to the general public; however, there remained a critical need for a nontechnical work on Oklahoma's cultural heritage. In 1997 I began work on a revision to *Oklahoma Prehistory* with the expectation that we could fund reprinting of an expanded version of Claudette's initial work, but increased printing costs made this impossible. In late 1997 the revised draft was submitted to the University of Oklahoma Press for consideration, and it was subsequently accepted for publication.

The second edition of *Oklahoma Prehistory* contains an edited version of Claudette Gilbert's original work and has been expanded to reflect the growing body of knowledge about Oklahoma's prehistory. This edition has been renamed *From Mounds to Mammoths* in order to reduce confusion with another book published for use in the college classroom, *The Prehistory of Oklahoma,* edited by Robert E. Bell.

I wish to thank the many people who have contributed their time and skills to this work. Many individuals assisted Claudette in the development of the first edition: Don Wyckoff helped in the research and editing; Larry Neal, David Hughes, Sarah Herstand, and Tim Baugh reviewed the text. Lois Albert helped with the discussion of palynology; Janet Black and Pam Odell typed the final draft of the first edition; and Tim Baugh and Rain Vehik patiently answered questions and helped with photos for the early buffalo hunter and forager chapters. Mary Goodman provided the beautiful drawings found throughout the first and second editions. Robert E. Bell reviewed the manuscript and patiently hunted down negatives, and J. Daniel Rogers helped with the chapter on Caddoan mound builders.

In the revisions and additions to this second edition, Lee Bement and Marjorie Duncan are responsible for the new information on Folsom and Calf Creek materials. Lee, Marjy, Lois Albert, and Richard Drass read or commented on the expanded sections for the new edition as well as on the previous version. Peter Tirrel and Judy Furlong Jordan of the Sam Noble Oklahoma Museum of Natural History assisted in the review of the first edition. I also wish to thank other members of the Oklahoma Archeological Survey staff for their help in bringing this publication to press.

I would like to acknowledge the Western History Collections, University of Oklahoma Libraries, and the Museum of the Great Plains in Lawton, Oklahoma, for granting use of their photo files and illustrations.

Towana Spivey, Steve Wilson, and Joe Anderson at the Museum of the Great Plains are to be thanked for their helpfulness.

A special thanks goes to the Peabody Museum of Archaeology and Ethnology at Harvard University for granting permission to use four illustrations of Spiro materials from *PreColumbian Shell Engravings* by Philip Phillips and James A. Brown. Richard C. Bartlett, Director of Publications at the time of the first edition, was most helpful in granting permission to use the illustrations, supplying the names of the illustrators, and encouraging the preparation of *Oklahoma Prehistory.* I wish to thank Donna Dickerson of the Peabody Museum for granting continued use of their materials in the second edition.

With the exception of the above noted materials, all illustrations are from the photo files of the Oklahoma Museum of Natural History and the Oklahoma Archeological Survey.

The Oklahoma Anthropological Society generously gave permission to use materials from their *Bulletin and Memoir* series. Others whose efforts are indispensable to the publication of this work are the editors at the University of Oklahoma Press, including Jean Hurtado and Sarah Nestor, and the Press's production staff. Finally, I wish to thank the archeological community and the dedicated members of the Oklahoma Anthropological Society, without whose efforts none of this would have been possible.

ROBERT L. BROOKS

May 1999

From Mounds to Mammoths

Introduction

Broken pots, discarded stone tools, charred plants, pollen, and bones—these are some of the bits and pieces archeologists use to reconstruct the past. Written history in Oklahoma goes back only a few centuries, and that record is often sketchy at best, but people have lived in the state for thousands of years. Through archeology, we can reconstruct their story.

Archeology is a branch of anthropology that studies people and cultures of the past. We learn about these people by examining the traces they have left of their passing, such as tools, buildings, and other artifacts. Many artifacts are beautiful and important as works of art; early archeologists, however, were interested in them primarily as a means of learning about the past. As the discipline matured, excavators demanded increasingly greater scientific detail. Modern archeologists carefully record information about the spatial relationship among artifacts, changes in soil color and texture, the function of built structures, and the many uses of tools, as well as many other factors.

The Lee Creek Ceremonial Center in northeastern Oklahoma is an excellent example of controlled excavation. The Lee Creek site was a regional ceremonial center whose people shared the same culture as those at the Spiro Mounds in eastern Oklahoma. Unlike Spiro, the site contained few prehistoric artifacts, and untrained excavators would have found little to interest them. But by carefully recording each change in the soil, the archeologists at the Lee Creek site were able to determine the sequence of events involved in mound construction.

Dating techniques have also markedly improved. In the 1950s radiocarbon dating came into use. All living things contain carbon, and after death, some of this carbon—the type called carbon 14—slowly disappears to re-form as nonradioactive nitrogen 14. Scientists learned how to measure the rate of this change and so to estimate the age of the organic (once living) material. The results of radiocarbon dating radically changed theories about when the first people reached the Americas. During the early part of this century, archeologists commonly believed that people entered the New World some four thousand or five thousand years ago. These estimates have gradually been pushed back as new information became available. With the advent of radiocarbon dating, some samples of organic material from the New World (such as charcoal and bone) that were tested yielded ages of ten thousand and even twenty thousand years old. The controversy still goes on, as even earlier dates have been obtained. Radiocarbon samples, however, are subject to contamination from many sources, and those samples that yield dates of more than ten thousand years old are carefully scrutinized.

In the meantime, scientists continue to search for other dating techniques that can be used to cross-check one another. Fluorine dating, archeomagnetism, and dendrochronology are just a few of these techniques. We may never know the complete story of Oklahoma's past people, but future research will continue to expand our knowledge.

This book is an attempt to bring together information from the many scientific journal articles, reports, and monographs written on the various aspects of Oklahoma archeology. We hope that you will find it an interesting and entertaining account of Oklahoma's prehistory.

Locations of some archeological sites in Oklahoma

1

Big-Game Hunters
25,000 B.C. to 5000 B.C.

The smell of damp earth and grass drifted down to him, mingling with the rank odor of mammoth. The steep-walled canyon was shady and cool after the long chase over the grassy plains. It was his first hunt, and he rubbed each sweaty palm in turn against his thigh to dry it, then gripped the spear tightly.

It was his best weapon, the wood smoothed straight and true with a sandstone abrader. He had painted the shaft with red ochre—the color of blood for luck. The point was made of finely chipped black flint mounted on a bone fore-shaft and set securely in a socket at the end of the spear shaft.

The wind shifted again and blew the hunters' scent toward the mammoth. Angrily, she shifted from foot to foot. Almost three times the height of a man, she paced back and forth, limping more than ever. It was probably from an old injury, the hunt leader had said. The old wound made her bad tempered, and her inability to get along with the other mammoths had forced her out of the herd. Alone, she had fallen prey to the small party of humans.

"Yaah!" yelled the hunt leader, and the men moved in, spears held for thrusting.

The mammoth trumpeted, raising curved tusks longer than a man was tall. Her long black hairs were dusty, and the yellow brown underwool was matted with mud. The wary hunter splashed through a small stream that ran along the bottom of the canyon and thrust at her bladder, hoping to poison her with her own urine. Others went for the eyes and the heart. The mammoth screamed and sank to her knees, blood streaming from half a dozen spear wounds. The young hunter pulled out his shaft and rammed another point into the socket. Slowly, the mammoth sank down onto her left side, her head facing north. The kill was soon over, and the hunters began butchering the huge carcass while a runner sped to the rest of the band with the good news.

Later, he sat by the fire, reworking a broken spearpoint. The hunting medicine had been very good this day. He had lost his first spearpoint somewhere in the giant carcass, but soon the band would pass the place where the red and white banded flint could be found, and he would make new spearpoints even more beautiful than the old.

The above scene is one that can be visualized from the archeological evidence found at the Domebo mammoth kill site in Caddo County, Oklahoma, some eleven thousand years ago.

Archeological discoveries in the 1990s have radically changed our interpretations of the antiquity of people in the New World. From a geological point of view, humans entered the New World in relatively recent times. Dinosaurs became extinct about 63 million

Possible Paleo-Indian migration routes, 25,000 [?] B.C. to 10,000 B.C.

years ago, but it was not until between twenty-five thousand and forty thousand years ago that the first people apparently reached the Americas. Archeologists call these first people Paleo-Indians, meaning "old Indians." There were several subgroups of these people, whose culture spread across all of the Americas and lasted several thousand years.

During the last ice age, glaciers covered much of the northern part of the world. They locked up huge amounts of water that remained frozen year-round. As the glaciers grew, the sea level dropped, which exposed many areas of land that are now covered by the oceans. One of these areas existed in the northern part of the Pacific Ocean called the Bering Strait, between Siberia and Alaska. By the late 1960s scientists called this land bridge "Beringia." At various times during the last ice age, the Bering Strait was a vast, dry plain with a narrow, ice-free corridor extending from the interior of Alaska into the heart of North America. At its widest point, Beringia was nearly one thousand miles across. It was easy for animals and the men and women who hunted them to drift across this vast span of dry land without ever realizing that they had moved from one continent to another.

Because of the extreme drop in sea levels caused by large amounts of water tied up in ice, it is possible that an ice-free area of land also existed connecting the east coast around Greenland and Iceland to Europe. There is speculation that some groups may possibly have entered the New World from northern Europe after traveling around this zone.

The first people to traverse this corridor and enter the New World were nomadic big-game hunters. They moved southward slowly, over a period of generations. There, they found an unpeopled new land with abundant game and plant foods.

The Earliest Natives of Oklahoma

One of the most spirited debates in archeology concerns how long ago people arrived in the New World. Some archeologists have challenged the long-held view that Clovis people were the earliest arrivals, some twelve thousand years ago. Using information from linguistics and DNA studies, they argue that Native Americans could have arrived some forty thousand to fifty thousand years ago. This is further substantiated by archeological investigations at the Monte Verde site in Chile. At Monte Verde, there is evidence of crude dwellings, a mammoth kill, and tools dating to some fourteen thousand years ago. Deeper but less conclusive cultural deposits at Monte Verde could date as early as thirty thousand years ago. Another intriguing site that may shed some light on these issues is the Burnham site in Woods County in northwestern Oklahoma. After the site was first reported in 1986, Don Wyckoff of the Oklahoma Archeological Survey spent six years excavating there with funds from the National Geographic Society, the National Science Foundation, and private donations. His work resulted in the discovery of a very ancient form of bison as well as many other animal species (mammoth, horse, short-faced bear, and American lion) that lived during the ice age. More importantly, about fifty flakes were found near the bison skull. The radiocarbon dates associated with the deposits containing the remains of these animals range from twenty-eight thousand to thirty-four thousand years ago, which could potentially represent the earliest evidence for people in North America. Unfortunately, it cannot be conclusively proven by the presence of the flakes that people were in Oklahoma at this early date. Work continues on this complex and very important archeological site.

The first well-documented Paleo-Indians are known to us as big-game hunters because they successfully hunted the gigantic game animals common during the last ice age. Huge bison, short-faced bears, mastodons, mammoths, and ground sloths the size of modern elephants were common. However, the Paleo-Indians of ten thousand years ago are best known for their mammoth and bison kills.

Mammoths are members of the elephant family. While a number of different species of mammoths roamed the North American plains at the time of the early Paleo-Indians, two commonly occurred in Oklahoma: Columbian mammoths and Imperial mammoths. The Columbian mammoth stood about fourteen feet high at the shoulder, while the average Imperial mammoth stood some three or four feet taller. Like modern elephants, mammoths probably lived in small family groups numbering no more than eight or ten animals: two or three adult females and their immature young. The males were probably solitary, as are modern male elephants.

Imperial Mammoth

Early Evidence for Big Game Hunters: The Cooperton Site

Radiocarbon dates obtained for the Cooperton site indicate that it is about seventeen thousand to twenty-one thousand years old. If this is correct, Cooperton provides some of the oldest evidence of human occupation in the state. However, due to disagreement over the reliability of bone-dating techniques, scientists have questioned the accuracy of these dates. The Cooperton site was discovered in 1961 and was excavated under the supervision of the Museum of the Great Plains in Lawton, Oklahoma. The excavators uncovered the bones of an immature male Columbian mammoth. Some of the bones, while still fresh, had been broken in a way that some scientists attribute to human activity. The archeologists who excavated the site also found three rounded, fist-sized rocks that they believe were used as hammerstones and a large fifteen-pound boulder that may have been used as an anvil by the prehistoric people who found the mammoth. While these items showed no clear evidence of intentional manufacture, both the hammerstones and the anvil were much larger than cobbles natural to the area, and any stream strong enough to have washed them to the site would also have washed away the mammoth bones.

The excavators believe that a small band of Paleo-Indians came upon a mammoth that had died of natural causes. The meat may have been spoiled, but the bone was useful for making tools. They also might have split the bones and set them in the sun in order to collect the liquid marrow that rose, as some African tribes do today with elephant bones. The bones may have been broken by putting them on a boulder carried to the site for that

Big-game hunters may have used these stones to break the bones of the Cooperton mammoth. Photo from Oklahoma Archeological Survey files, taken by permission at the Museum of the Great Plains.

purpose and then pounding them with the hammerstones. This would result in a break with jagged, sawtoothed edges like those found at the Cooperton site. If the bones had been broken by pressure from the weight of the ground after they were buried, they would have broken in a smoother line.

Early Big-Game Hunters: The Clovis People

Archeologists named the mammoth hunters the Clovis people after the Clovis site in New Mexico where their artifacts were first reported. According to the archeological evidence, mammoths were important to the

Clovis people, but the kills were infrequent. However, we now know that Clovis people not only hunted mammoths and other game but also collected edible wild plants. Mammoth hunting was probably done by small groups of men with stone-tipped spears. Nearly all organic materials from this time have long since decayed, especially in the warm, humid regions. Most of the remaining evidence of their life-style comes from objects made of stone. The Clovis people made many types of stone tools—scrapers, drills, and knives—but they are best known for their spearpoints.

Clovis spearpoints are typically three to four inches long. They are thin and leaf shaped and usually have one or more long flakes removed from the base toward the center, creating a channel or flute. Such points were used for spears, not arrows. The Clovis people did not make bows and arrows.

Spearpoints may have been fastened to the shaft in one of two ways. The hunters may have hafted the spearpoint to a bone foreshaft and then set the foreshaft in a socket in the wooden spearshaft. Using this method, a hunter could thrust rapidly and repeatedly. A bag containing spearpoints mounted on bone foreshafts would have been easy to carry. Another method of hafting was to tie the spearpoint directly onto the wooden spear shaft. This method would have been useful for inflicting repeated shallow wounds or for killing smaller game.

Isolated Clovis points have been found in many places in the state. Without accompanying datable materials, however, no age can be assigned to them, and they tell us little about the prehistoric big-game hunters. There are also finds of mammoth skeletons, but most of these had natural deaths, telling us nothing about the people in the region at the time. In Oklahoma, our

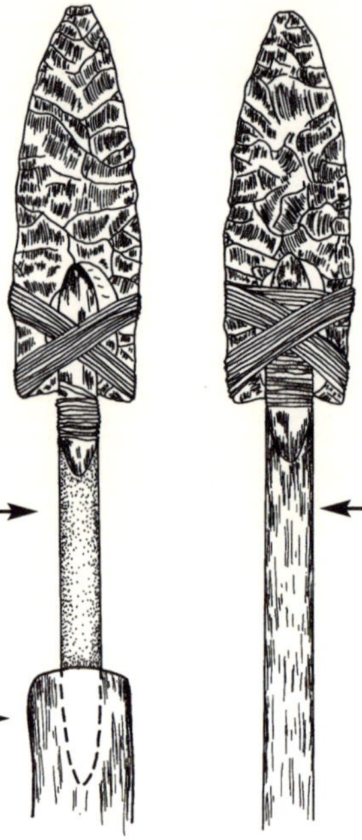

Two possible methods of mounting spearpoints

information about this period comes from one thoroughly studied site: the Domebo site in Caddo County.

The Domebo Site

An important site that yielded both mammoth bones and carefully made Clovis spearpoints is the Domebo (Dum.bo) mammoth kill site in Caddo County near Anadarko. The area is a flat prairie plain with many small streams cutting steep canyons into the sandstone bedrock. In 1961 J. E. "Buck" Patterson of Apache, Oklahoma, noticed a mammoth tusk eroding out of a stream bank in one of the narrow canyons. Patterson reported the find to Adrian D. Anderson, then an archeologist at the Museum of the Great Plains at Lawton. When Anderson examined the site, he found a Clovis spearpoint with the mammoth bones. He knew at once that it was an important discovery. Mammoths had been extinct for some ten thousand years. This meant that the site was more than ten thousand years old, and the spearpoint found with it was probably the oldest indisputable evidence for the presence of people in Oklahoma. A National Science Foundation Emergency Grant was secured, and excavation began in 1962.

Because of the possible association of a Clovis spearpoint with the mammoth remains, the context of the Domebo site was extremely important. The excavators were concerned with the relative positions of each of the features and artifacts of the site. A Clovis point by itself cannot be dated; mammoth bones alone may not tell us anything about the people of the time; but together, they provide important information. Therefore, the excavators were careful to note the exact position of all the remains. In order to keep a precise, three-dimensional record, the site was first marked off in a grid of equal squares. The squares were measured with reference to a central point, which kept the grid formed by the squares uniform. The grid made it possible to map the surface of the site. For a three-dimensional record, however, measuring depth was also important. Depth is recorded in "levels," which may be either arbitrary or natural. When measuring in arbitrary levels, the archeologist decides that a certain number of inches or centimeters will be dug to best expose a level. All the levels will be the same depth. Natural levels, on the other hand, are based on changes in soil color and texture that the archeologist uses to demarcate the different levels. The excavators at the Domebo site used arbitrary levels.

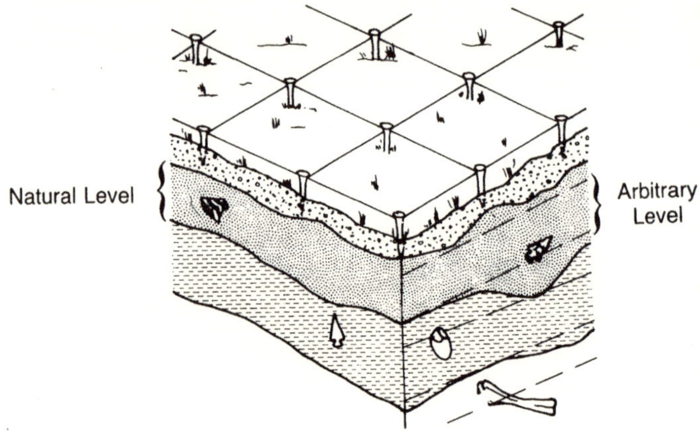

Context: The relationship of each part to other parts of the site

The Domebo skeleton proved to be that of an immature female Columbian mammoth. She stood about fourteen feet high at the shoulder. With her bones, the excavators found two complete spearpoints, one spearpoint fragment, and three waste flakes. Another spearpoint, a scraper, and a worked flake were found in the gravel downstream from the excavation.

Flint Knapping

The waste flakes indicated that one of the hunters had made or retouched a tool while the group camped nearby. Before metal became generally used, people made their tools from stone, wood, and bone. The early stone tools were made by a technique archeologists call "flint knapping." The flint knapper struck chips from the stone being made into a tool with another stone (a hammerstone) or with a piece of bone or antler (a billet). The tools were made from different varieties of flint and chert, quartzite, and, occasionally, obsidian (a volcanic glass). Most of the Clovis-period artifacts are made of flint. The spearpoints show especially great refinement and skill.

When a piece of flint or chert is struck from above at the correct angle, a shock wave travels through the stone and causes a flake to detach. Archeologists have discovered that there were two basic techniques used to make flaked stone tools. In one technique, pieces of the original stone, called a core, are removed until the tool reaches the desired shape. Archeologists refer to tools made in this way as "core tools."

In the second technique, the flint knapper makes finished tools from the flakes chipped off the core. These

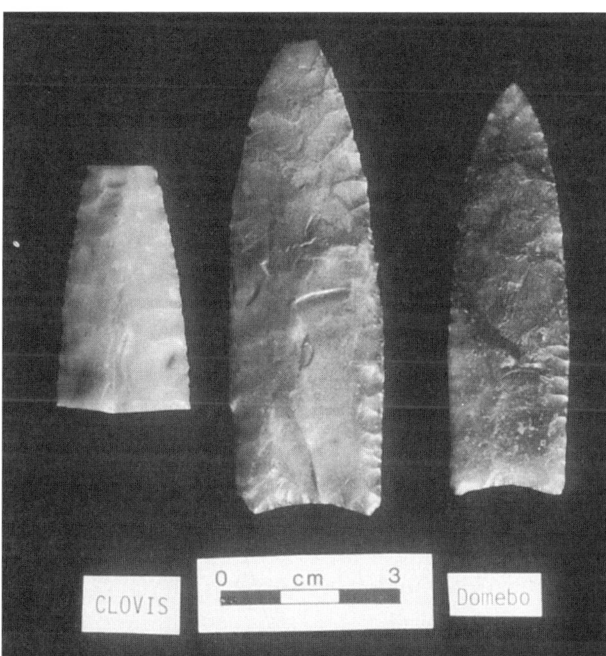

Three points found at the Domebo site. Photo courtesy of the Museum of the Great Plains.

flakes may be used as they are, or they may be retouched or reshaped. Retouching requires a great deal of skill. The flakes can be knapped with a hammerstone or with a bone or antler striker for finer flaking. Even more delicate finishing work can be done along the edges by pressure flaking. In pressure flaking, the flake is pressed off with pressure from the bone or antler flaker rather than struck off.

Fossil Pollen

Samples of soil and clay (called "sediment") were collected when the Domebo site was excavated. A palynologist (a person who studies pollen) examined these sediments in order to learn more about the fossil pollen present in them. Fossil pollen can provide information about the environment at the time of the kill. Trees, grasses, and other plants produce millions of pollen grains each year. Plants whose pollen is carried by the wind spreads much more pollen than the pollen spread by plants using insects or animal carriers. A percentage of these grains are buried in the annual accumulation of sediment. The pollen of most plants is very resistant to decay if buried under the right conditions. The type of soil in which pollen is buried is important as well, since pollen is best preserved in soil containing either a large quantity of water or no water at all and in a clayey rather than a sandy soil. Air that reaches pollen causes it to decay more rapidly. Some kinds of pollen grains preserve better than others because they have thicker, more resistant walls.

There is almost as much variation among pollen grains as there is among their parent plants. Thus, it is possible to tell what kinds of plants produced the pollen and to estimate whether many or few of them were growing in the area. Knowledge of the kinds of plants growing near a site at the time it was occupied can provide information about the climate, since different kinds of plants grow in various climates.

By looking at the pollen samples recovered from the Domebo site, the palynologist learned that the climate was about 10° cooler in the summer and 10° warmer in the winter at the time of the kill than it is in present-day Oklahoma. Across the state, there was less variation in rainfall and temperature than there is now, with more trees and plenty of lush grassland.

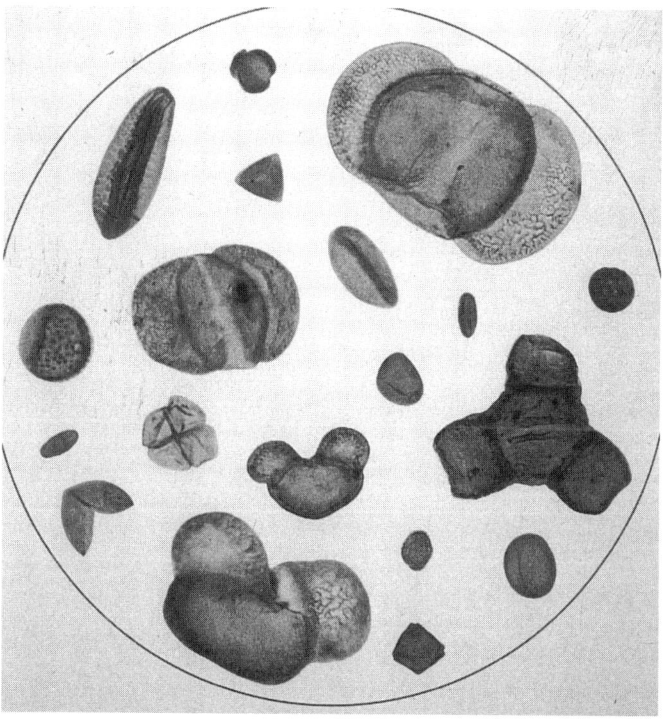

Pollen types important for vegetational and environmental change

Later Big-Game Hunters: The Folsom People

By around ten thousand years ago most mammoths were extinct, although some populations survived for two thousand to three thousand years longer in Florida, South America, and the Aleutian Islands. Though no one knows why mammoths became extinct, it has been suggested that changes in climate at the end of the ice age and overhunting may have been contributing factors. Early hunters then turned to the giant forms of bison as their main source of meat. These Paleo-Indian bison hunters lived approximately ten thousand years ago.

Folsom people hunted an ancestor of the modern bison or buffalo called *Bison antiquus.* These bison were between 25 and 30 percent larger than modern bison and correspondingly heavier. A modern buffalo bull weighs about 1,800 pounds and a cow about 700 to 1,200

Prehistoric bison

pounds. An extinct giant bison bull, in comparison, probably weighed some 2,250 pounds and a cow around 1,000 pounds.

Lacking horses (which also became extinct in North America at the end of the ice age), the Folsom people hunted bison on foot—a dangerous and tricky undertaking. They frequently used either the surround or the mass drive hunting technique or a combination of the two. In a surround the animals are encircled by the hunters, who close in slowly, driving the game towards the center of the circle. The animals are unable to break through the human fence for fear of the people. Bunched together in the trap, they are easily killed by the hunters. In a drive the animals are stampeded over a cliff or into a natural feature such as a canyon.

Individual or small group hunts also went on throughout the prehistoric past at the same time as the communal hunts. The mass hunt depended upon the availability of a herd of bison, the presence of a natural trap or a human-made corral, and a band of hunters large enough to force a controlled stampede.

As soon as the bison were killed, the hunters butchered them. Spoilage begins immediately after death, so in warm weather speed was important. The hunters often used heavy choppers and even the bones and hooves of the bison themselves. Bone from a freshly killed animal is very tough, much stronger than bone that has dried, and makes a good butchering tool.

The most extensive research on the late big-game hunters has been done in Wyoming and Colorado; however, the Cooper Bonebed site, a bison kill, has been studied in Harper County and the Waugh site, a possible camp from this period, has been found near Laverne, also in Harper County.

The later big-game hunters used spears in hunting, as had the Clovis people before them. Folsom spearpoints are even more finely flaked than Clovis points, with many of them made from a type of chert or flint found in south-central Texas. The flint knappers fabricated many other types of tools as well. Archeologists have found knives, hide scrapers, drills, and awls. Most of these tools were used in the processing of large game animals such as the buffalo.

The buffalo—as it is commonly called—is, in fact, the American bison. Bison are among an order of paired hooved grass eaters including cattle, sheep, and goats. Numerous species of bison have lived in North America since their evolution during the ice ages. There were two types of historic bison: the woods and plains bison. Since the appearance of people in North America, bison have provided a variety of resources for Native Americans, including food, bone for tools and ornaments, hide for clothing and shelter, and internal organs for storage and hide tanning. Overall, more than one hundred different uses of bison have been documented, prompting archeologists to call them "Oklahoma's First General Store."

While large numbers of Folsom spearpoints have been found across western Oklahoma, the Cooper Bonebed in Harper County is one of only two sites at which Folsom artifacts occur in a datable context and are associated with other materials. Based on the age of other sites of the Folsom culture on the southern plains, the Cooper Bonebed dates from between 10,200 and 10,800 years ago. The site is located on an old filled-in gully on the north side of the North Canadian or Beaver River. For many years, local residents had observed bones eroding from the bank. However, it was not until November 22, 1992, that the location was visited by an archeologist, Lee Bement of the Oklahoma Archeological Survey. Bement recognized the bones as those of *Bison antiquus,* an extinct species of bison. During this initial visit, the remains of a substantial number of animals were recorded, but no artifacts were found. The Cooper Bonebed was revisited several times by archeologists from the Survey, and in the spring of 1993, a fragmented Folsom spearpoint was found. The presence of the Folsom point clearly established the Cooper Bonebed as a bison kill dating to some ten thousand years ago. More importantly, it was only the second Folsom site recorded for Oklahoma. Led by Bement, excavations were conducted in 1993 and 1994 with funds provided by the National Geographic Society and private donations.

Excavations at the Cooper Bonebed yielded extremely important information about the hunting behavior of the Folsom people and the animals they hunted. Three separate kill episodes were documented as having taken place in the gully or arroyo. The upper and middle kills contained twenty-nine animals, while

Uppermost bison kill at the Cooper site in Harper County

the lower kill contained twenty animals. In many cases, the remains are complete and intact (articulated) bison skeletons. An additional thirty animals were found in an area that had eroded and lay below the kill location. The site represents one of the largest collections of *Bison antiquus* skeletons and provides excellent opportunities to learn more about this extinct species.

Over thirty Folsom spearpoints were recovered in the excavations. One of the more fascinating aspects of these spearpoints concerns the stone from which they were manufactured. The two most common materials were a dark gray flint found near Austin, Texas, and a red and white banded material found near Amarillo, Texas. Another Folsom spearpoint was made of a yellow jasper that came from northwestern Kansas. This wide distribution of materials suggests highly mobile hunting groups, roaming over an area of almost a thousand miles. The tools made from these stones were highly valued. When they were at a considerable distance from the sources of the stones, they would continually resharpen and rework broken tools rather than search for a nearby and lesser quality material with which they were unfamiliar. As a result, approximately 90 percent of the spearpoints were made of these materials.

Perhaps the most startling find of the Cooper Bonebed excavations was the discovery in the lower kill of a red zigzag (lighting bolt) painted on the front part of a bison skull. The skull represents the earliest painted art in North America and clear evidence that hunting practices of the Folsom people also involved other parts of their culture, such as ritual.

While Folsom and other specialized hunters inhabited western Oklahoma, people in the eastern wood-

Folsom spearpoints found at the Cooper site

Bison skull from Cooper site with painted zigzag representing what is believed to be the earliest artwork in North America. Oklahoma Archeological Survey Photo Files.

lands of the state were living a somewhat different existence. The Dalton people, who lived throughout much of eastern Oklahoma some nine thousand to ten thousand years ago, had a way of life focused on the hunting of deer and other game animals and the collecting of edible wild plants. This is in marked contrast to the lifestyle of bison-hunting groups in the west. These early natives also appear to have lived in slightly larger groups or bands than their western counterparts.

Gradually, the ways of life of the bison hunters and hunter/collectors changed. As their populations increased and the environment became warmer and drier, prehistoric groups roamed over increasingly smaller territories and adopted new ways of life, ushering in a new era: the time of the foragers.

2

The Foragers

5,000 B.C. to A.D. 1

The young girl and her mother rose early and left their hut of grass and branches. They soon joined other women and children of the band, and the noisy group strolled slowly toward the stand of blackberry bushes. After half an hour's walk, they came to the spot where the fat, dark berries hung thickly on the briars. The girl reached out eagerly, filling her mouth first, then dropping berries into the skin bag her mother had given her to fill.

"A bear! A bear!" cried one of the children. Mothers snatched up their babies and the older children tugged along their little brothers and sisters. They hurried back to the camp. When they reached the temporary huts, they found only two of the band's twelve hunters seated by the fireside.

"There's a bear among the blackberries," one of the women said, "a big, brown bear!"

The men quickly put down the stone tools they had been sharpening. They gathered up their darts and atlatls (dart throwers). The women and children talked excitedly.

The hunters would surely make their kill, and the whole band would feast on bear meat tonight.

A scene such as this possibly took place at the Lawrence site in Nowata County, Oklahoma, around 2,700 years ago.

The foragers were hunters, like the people before them, but they hunted modern species of game. In eastern Oklahoma deer were an important source of meat, while buffalo were hunted in the western part of the state. Because of increasing populations and conflicts with their neighboring groups, however, the foragers ranged over a more restricted territory and made more intensive use of local natural resources than the people before them had done. During this time Oklahoma vegetation also attained its historic character, resulting in an environment quite different from that present at the end of the ice age. In season, the foragers gathered nuts, berries, seeds, and roots. They crushed the hard-shelled plant foods in grinding basins made of sandstone. These basins were small, with a shallow depression where the grinding stone was rubbed over the seeds and nuts in a circular motion. The foragers used wooden digging sticks with fire-hardened tips, and they made baskets, nets, and string from plant fibers and long, stringy roots. By the time of the foragers, dogs had also been domesticated and had become a familiar part of camp life.

Ground Stone Tools

Items such as axes and atlatl weights were made of pecked and ground stone. Pecking, a new tool-making technique, consisted of a series of rapid blows with a hammerstone to the surface of the artifact that removed small fragments of stone. After the artifact was pecked into shape, its final form was completed by grinding, which was done using an abrasive such as sandstone or sand along with water. Water was very important to the process, because it kept the abrasive particles suspended. The artifact was ground until it was smooth, and it may sometimes have received a final polishing with clay or a piece of hide. Other artifacts such as grinding basins and manos (hand-held grinding stones) were pecked into shape, their final shaping the result of use rather than intentional manufacture.

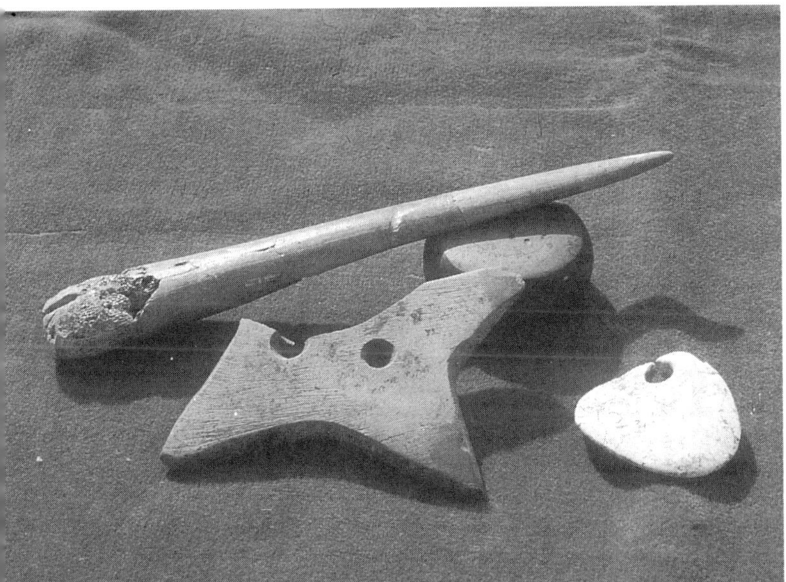

Ground stone, shell, and bone artifacts from the forager period (not to scale). Oklahoma Archeological Survey Photo Files.

▲▲▲▲

The first widespread evidence of the atlatl, or dart thrower, appears during this period. Atlatls were short spears made of wood, with a bone or antler hook at the end to keep the dart from sliding out. They were usually about eighteen inches long and had a groove down the center in which the dart rested. Atlatls were sometimes weighted with ground stone weights to give more force to the thrust. An atlatl, which functions like an extension of the arm, allowed the hunter to throw his dart further and more accurately. Spear shafts were generally about forty-eight inches long, while dart shafts were about thirty-six inches long. The points of both weapons were alike. The advantage of the atlatl to the prehistoric hunter was that the shorter length of the dart shaft allowed him to carry a larger supply of darts with greater ease.

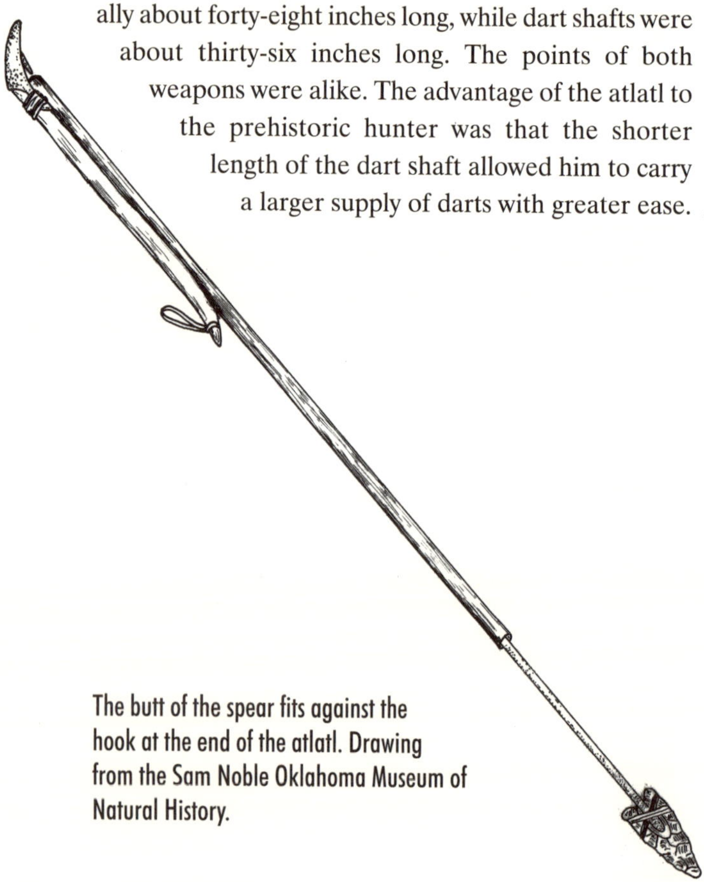

The butt of the spear fits against the hook at the end of the atlatl. Drawing from the Sam Noble Oklahoma Museum of Natural History.

Hunters in eastern Oklahoma usually took their deer in single kills, but in western Oklahoma herds of buffalo were killed by bands of hunters. The buffalo were driven into narrow, closed canyons where the hunters speared the animals as they milled in a compact group.

Calf Creek Culture

While small groups of foraging people were establishing themselves across Oklahoma, the climate was dramatically changing. Between seven thousand and four thousand years ago, much of the state experienced warmer conditions and drought unparalleled in modern times. Remarkably, native peoples adapted to their harsh surroundings, living in highly mobile bands. One such group, distinguished by their finely made spearpoints, was called the Calf Creek culture. People of this culture lived throughout Oklahoma and the Southern Plains region some five thousand to six thousand years ago. They hunted bison as well as a variety of smaller game animals, supplementing their meat diet with edible starchy plant seeds that they gathered. The seeds were probably made more readily available by the drier conditions. Their tools consisted of large spearpoints, knives and scrapers for butchering of game and hide processing, and more exotic pieces such as notching flakes. These flakes were used by Calf Creek people to experiment with the manufacture of deep hafting notches like those found on these pieces. The Calf Creek spearpoints are large, with notches in the base. Because of the large size of the points, most camps of the people who made them contain large quantities

Calf Creek spearpoint from Haskell County

of thin flakes resulting from the production of these tools. A few grinding stones used in plant-seed processing have also been found in the camps.

Due to the severity of environmental conditions during the time of the foragers, the integrity of most Calf Creek sites has been seriously damaged by erosion in the ensuing thousand years, and only limited insights are available concerning these people's way of life. They apparently lived in small temporary camps and favored locations with commanding views. It appears that four groups of Calf Creek people lived in the east central, north central, south central, and western areas of the state. These groups made use of high-quality flint found in the four areas, frequently heating the stone to improve its flaking properties. People of the Calf Creek culture are also known to have left caches of flint stored in the ground for future retrieval and use.

View from the Anthony site, a Calf Creek site in Caddo County. Note the surrounding vista that would have been seen by Calf Creek people.

In 1989 a farmer in Caddo County contacted the Archeological Survey about the large number of spearpoints he had collected from a ridgetop on his property. Upon inspection these were found to be Calf Creek spearpoints. In addition, his collection included numerous other tools such as scrapers, drills, and wedges. Examination of the ridgetop resulted in the discovery of numerous flakes, principally products of the resharpening of knives and spearpoints. Remarkably, most of the flakes were made of flint from areas where the four groups of Calf Creek people lived. This suggests that the Anthony site served as a gathering place for Calf Creek people. Such locations were valuable for exchanging information, finding marriage partners, trading, and performing religious ceremonies.

OTHER FORAGING GROUPS: THE GORE PIT SITE

In addition to the Calf Creek culture, other foraging societies roamed across the Oklahoma landscape. The foragers followed a seasonal round, their movements and the number of people in the group determined by the available food supply. They used the same campsites year after year as each area's special harvest became available. To cook their food, they often built rock-lined fireplaces or roasting pits.

Archeologists have found evidence of this cooking technique at the Gore Pit site in Comanche County. There, archeologists, aided by Oklahoma Anthropological Society members, found several burned rock and

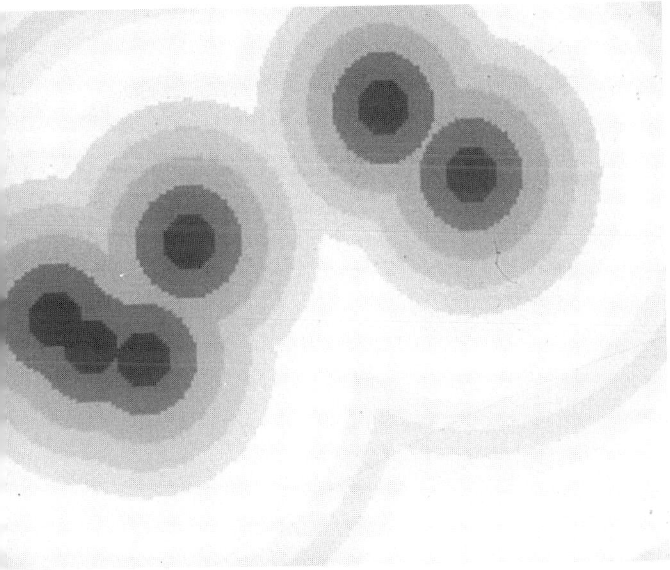

Distribution of chipped-stone tool-making debris at the Anthony site, using Graphic Information System (GIS) analysis.

charcoal concentrations. A scatter of burned rocks, mussel shells, animal bones, and ash surrounded the cooking pits.

Some six thousand years ago, people at this site camped near a small spring where they dug shallow pits six to eight feet across. They piled wood in the pits and burned it down to coals, then placed rocks on top of the coals. They put the food to be cooked on top of the rocks, piled more rocks and earth over it, and left this oven until everything was fully baked. Then they threw aside the top layer and removed the food, leaving behind evidence of their activity in the form of burned rock and charcoal layers in the soil.

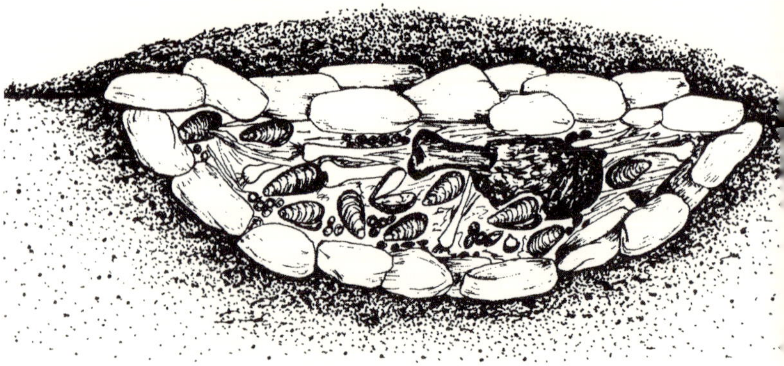

Profile of a rock oven. The foragers used rock ovens of various kinds to bake their food.

Excavations at the Gore Pit site, Caddo County. Photo courtesy of the Museum of the Great Plains.

Some foraging groups in northeastern Oklahoma used caves or bluff shelters for their camping places. The shelters exist where there is enough overhang to protect an area five to fifteen feet deep at the base of the cliff. They are generally well drained and protected from wind. The same factors that made the shelters choice living quarters also protected the debris left by the foragers, often providing excellent records of life during this period. Over the years, the trash discarded at the shelters accumulated as thick layers of soil containing broken bone, bits of stone, ash, and broken tools. If

Rock shelter in Delaware County

these sites are left undisturbed by vandals or erosion, careful excavation by trained researchers can provide a precise record of the activities that took place in them.

Human Biology

Some human burials of foragers have been found in Oklahoma, the skeletons providing information about how these people looked, lived, and died. The earliest burial for this period in Oklahoma, discovered in Comanche County, was radiocarbon dated at 7,100 years ago. The skeleton of a woman was found lying on its side in a flexed position, the arms together in front, the legs bent, and the head bent towards the knees. This position is common in many prehistoric burials, although some people buried their dead fully extended. There were no grave goods with the burial. The presence of two fractures on the woman's skull suggest a violent death.

Other skeletons from eastern Oklahoma are from 3,400 to 2,000 years old. These people were shorter than the average height today (approximately five feet two inches to five feet five inches). On the average, men were about thirty-five years old when they died, while women usually died at a slightly younger age. Some individuals suffered from decayed teeth and arthritis. There was also evidence of disease, although the exact causes of death are unknown. There were also skeletons with bones that had been broken but had healed while the person was still alive.

In Oklahoma the population continued to grow slowly, the people engaging in trade as well as in conflicts with neighboring groups. They began to build semipermanent houses and to become more sedentary, due to less ability to move across the land because of the competition for land due to an increase in population. By the end of this important period of transition, the people had developed pottery and incipient horticulture. This led to the rise of early farming communities in Oklahoma.

3

Early Farmers

A.D. 1 to A.D. 1000

The young man pounded the pole into the ground while his brother held it upright. He used a round stone as a hammer, and the repeated "chuck, chuck" was a rhythmic background to the other noises the family made as they helped to build the new house. He stopped to wipe the sweat from his face with a forearm tanned dark brown from a life lived mostly out of doors. His wife-to-be smiled at him from across the way, where she was helping to dig a storage pit. He smiled back, then returned to work. Soon, the two of them would share this house together.

This scene was one that occurred at many archeological sites in central and eastern Oklahoma some two thousand years ago.

About two thousand years ago in central and eastern Oklahoma, farming began to replace the foraging way of life. The early farmers lived in semipermanent houses and stayed in the same place long enough to raise a crop of pigweed, goosefoot, squash, and sunflowers. They lived in small hamlets of two or three houses, each occupied by members of an extended family, including parents, grandparents, brothers, sisters, aunts, uncles, and cousins. The early farmers also took game from nearby hunting areas and continued to gather wild plants.

In the New World, farming began as early as four thousand to seven thousand years ago. Important native-food plants, including corn, beans, squash, and chiles, were domesticated far to the south of Oklahoma in Mexico, Central America, and South America. In this early farming period, one thousand to two thousand years ago, sunflower, native squash/gourd, may grass, marsh elder, and goosefoot and pigweed (chenopods) were domesticated in North America. The early farmers' fields were more like family garden plots than like the large-scale efforts of modern farmers. Early farmers did all their cultivating by hand, using wooden digging sticks and hoes with flint or bone blades. They planted their crops in clusters, so that tending and harvesting was easier.

Seeds of these native Oklahoma plants were rich in carbohydrates and vitamins. Most of the plants, such as sunflower, goosefoot, and pigweed, were harvested in the fall after the seeds had ripened and dried. Workers then ground the seeds into a meal or pastelike substance, using rough-surfaced grinding stones and sandstone basins.

Archeologists cannot yet determine who Oklahoma's first prehistoric farmers were. It appears that farming was adopted at about the same time in a number of diverse regions of Oklahoma, including the Grand River region in northeastern Oklahoma, the Ouachita Mountains in the southeastern part of the state, the area along the Canadian and Washita Rivers in central and western Oklahoma, and the Cimarron River area in the Oklahoma panhandle. In northeastern Oklahoma, the people made pottery and stone tools that looked like those made by the early farming people of western Missouri. Either some of the Missouri people moved to Oklahoma to live, or some of the Oklahoma foragers in the northeastern part of the state learned about farming from their neighbors in Missouri.

Early farmers ground corn and other foods in sandstone grinding basins. Photo from Oklahoma Archeological Survey Files.

Pottery, or the idea of making it, probably came from both the eastern and the southwestern United States. The foragers used skin bags and baskets because they were lightweight and durable—important considerations for nomadic people who had to carry all their household goods with them as they traveled to areas where game and plant foods were seasonally available. But as people settled in permanent dwellings, pottery became more practical.

Clay is easily worked into a variety of shapes. Temper is usually added to the clay before shaping, so that the vessel will not break during firing. The early potters used ground bone, sand, ground shell, and other materials as temper. Once the clay is fired, it becomes pottery—a material with new properties. Baking the clay at high temperatures causes chemical changes, resulting in a pot that is hard, capable of holding water, and very resistant to heat.

Pottery making was traditionally women's work among historic Native American societies, so archeologists think that the early prehistoric potters were also women. Pottery is brittle, but the broken pieces, the potsherds, may last for thousands of years. We know about the type of pottery made during this period because of the potsherds that have been found. Archeologists seldom find a whole pot or even enough sherds from the same pot to reconstruct it. The pots may have been broken and discarded, as we throw away broken dishes today. Natural forces such as pressure may also have further broken them in the ground. Some societies ritually "killed" vessels used in burials and ceremonies by knocking a hole in them. In modern times construction machinery destroys many artifacts, and treasure hunters break them and scatter the pieces with their careless, unscientific digging. Despite these problems, archeologists have found enough evidence to learn how the early farmers made their vessels.

The potters used a coiling technique. They rolled the clay out in ropes, then coiled them, one layer on top of the other, to form the body of the pot, pinching the coils together as they worked. Some potters set the base of the pot in a basket or gourd while working. When the clay cured enough to be firm but was not fully dried, the potter often finished the pot by cord marking. Using a smooth rock in one hand and a cord-wrapped paddle in the other, she beat the outside of the pot with the paddle. The rock she held on the inside supported

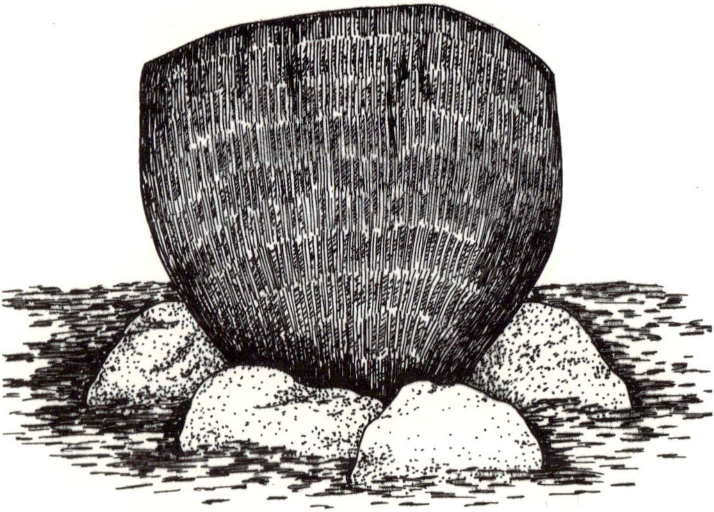

Early farmers' pots must have been propped up to stay upright.

the wall of the pot as she pounded, keeping it from collapsing.

Sometimes, the pots were also decorated with simple designs around the rim. Archeologists are not sure why the women cord marked their pots. The pounding thinned the walls of the pot, making it lighter weight for its size, and it also sealed the coils together more firmly. These may have been considerations. On the other hand, the women may simply have liked the decorative effect of the cord marking. Archeologists can frequently determine the "what" and "how" of the past, but the "why" is much more difficult to answer.

The first pots were simple and utilitarian. Photo from Oklahoma Archeological Survey Files.

The early pots were shaped much like the baskets and skin bags that had been used earlier. They were usually oval or egg shaped, with the bottoms pointed or rounded, so that the pots needed to be propped up to stay upright. When they were used, some pots were undoubtedly stabilized with rocks or lumps of clay in the fire, or a pot's bottom was set in a hole, with hot coals piled around the sides. In other cases, the pots were placed on clay tripods during cooking.

Tools

While the women made pottery, the men made tools of stone and wood. Axes of chipped and ground stone were used to cut down trees, to make temporary shelters, and to create wooden tools. One type of ax is called a grooved ax because of the groove around its center that was an aid in attaching the ax head to the handle. The early farmers also made double-bitted axes (with a cutting edge at both ends) and adzes. An adz, unlike an ax, is fastened to the handle at a right angle, so that the cutting blade can be used with a hoeing-like motion, making it useful for jobs such as hollowing out logs. The early farmers also made celts of polished and ground stone. The celts were like small axes, usually about four to six inches long and one or two inches wide. They were smooth in the middle, with no groove for attaching a handle, and may have been used like wedges to aid in splitting wood.

Village Life

By A.D. 500, there were small farming villages along the Arkansas, Verdigris, and Grand Rivers and their tributaries; some two hundred years later, villages were to be found as far south as the Arbuckle Mountains. The early farmers selected places of mixed forest and prairie in which to live. Their hamlets were located in fertile valleys where the soil was easy to till using tools of wood, bone, and stone. The open prairies were unsuitable for early farming techniques, because the grasses growing on them set down long, tough roots through the sod, making the soil too difficult to till with aboriginal tools. It was not until modern times when metal plow blades became widely available that farming on the upland prairies became practical. The early farmers used the open prairies principally as a hunting ground for deer, bison, and other game.

Houses

The early farmers' houses, while more elaborate than any shelters built previously, were still lightly constructed, easily assembled buildings. The farmers drove poles into the ground to form a framework, which was covered with grass thatch or cane matting to form the walls. The people made circular hearths out of limestone or other rock and dug shallow, basin-shaped pits that they used for storage and for trash. A few artifacts, burned rocks from hearths, stains of filled-in postholes, and shallow trash pits may be all that remain to mark the location of an early farmers' hamlet. By careful study of such clues, archeologists can reconstruct what life was like for people living in Oklahoma some two thousand years ago.

4

Plains Village Farmers

A.D. 800 to A.D. 1400

The heat made sweat run down her back and gather at the waist of her skin skirt. She ignored it, skillfully using her bone-tipped digging stick to dig out the weeds that threatened to strangle the young corn. Already, it grew as high as her knees, and the tender bean plants looped over it like a necklace. The gourds grew well, too. They would have a good harvest this year. Some years, there was too little rain. Then the crops died in the fields and the people faced hardship.

Nearby, in the shade cast by the wall of the house, her mother and aunts were making clay pots. They had dug clay from the riverbank and brought it home to make big round-bottomed cooking pots. The rest of the extended family had gone to hunt buffalo. When they returned, there would be fresh meat to eat and dry, hides to tan, and bone to be made into tools. In the meantime, there was the garden.

This particular scene was replayed countless times at sites such as Heerwald in Custer County about seven hundred to nine hundred years ago.

Because of a more stable food supply brought about by the introduction of corn, beans, and tropical squash from Mexico by about twelve hundred years ago, the early farmers' population expanded. By A.D. 800 farming societies had spread into the plains of north central and western Oklahoma. They continued to build their villages along river valleys, where the soil was easily cultivated. The remains of these villages have been found along the major rivers and their principal tributaries in the region, including the Arkansas, Canadian, North Canadian, Washita, and Red Rivers.

Though some of the corn was eaten while it was green during late June and early July, most was allowed to become fully mature and dry on the cob before it was harvested. The dried corn could be kept for long periods of time and provided food throughout the winter. The hard kernels of dried corn were made into meal by first being shattered with a hammerstone and then being ground with a mano (grinding stone) and metate (trough-shaped grinding basin).

The Plains Village farmers of central and western Oklahoma had to contend with a drier and more variable climate than did the people living to the east. Although moister conditions prevailed between A.D. 1000 and A.D. 1300, drought and violent storms were common. The area was mostly tallgrass prairie, with a few trees growing near the streams. The people grew crops in gardenlike plots, hunted local game, and occasionally fished. Archeologists have found the remains of corn, beans, and gourds, and the farmers probably also grew squash, sunflowers, and tobacco. The women apparently tended the crops; hoes and digging sticks have been found in some women's graves, but none have yet been found in men's graves. The men are thought to have been the hunters, since spears and arrowpoints have been found in their graves. A similar sex-based division of labor was common among historic Native Americans.

Deer and buffalo supplied most of the meat, hides, and bones for tools and ornaments. The hunters also killed elk, antelope, wolf, badger, coyote, raccoon, beaver, lynx, opossum, rabbit, squirrel, and other game. They hunted wild turkeys and ducks, and they took fish,

White-tailed deer

Wild turkey

turtles, and mussels from the rivers. The hunters used bows and arrows and spears, as well as traps, snares, deadfalls, and pits. There is no evidence of the large bison kills common during the time of the big game hunters and foragers, so hunting was likely done by small groups of men.

The bow and arrow was adopted during the period of the early farmers, but it was probably not until the time of the Plains Village farmers that it was widely used by hunters. This weapon gave hunters an important advantage, allowing them to hunt game from greater distances. Also, one or two hunters were more likely to be successful than were the many men needed to drive animals to a location where they could be killed with a spear.

The women planted their crops near the villages, tending them with tools of bone and wood. Digging sticks were made from buffalo leg bones, hoe blades from buffalo shoulder blades or skulls, and sickles from deer jaws. The Plains Village farmers also gathered many wild plants for food, dyes, and medicine. Hickory nuts and walnuts, hackberry seeds, wild cherries, plums, persimmons, and many other plants grew nearby. Corn and seeds were ground in milling basins, and mortars were used to crush plant foods such as nuts.

Food was stored in underground cache pits that were larger and deeper than those dug by the early farmers—three to five feet deep and three to five feet wide. The cache pits probably functioned like root cellars, keeping the dried corn and other food cool and sealing it off from scavengers. Eventually, insects and other vermin penetrated the pits, making them no longer useful for storage. The pits were subsequently used as places for dumping trash and debris.

The women cooked over fireplaces, both indoors and out of doors. Interior fireplaces, which were better made and show more signs of use, provided heat and light as well as a place for cooking. Much of the food was cooked in pottery vessels. Many of the pot sherds from village sites of this period have a thin, carbonized layer on the outside of the sherd, demonstrating that pots were placed directly over or in the fire. These pots, made by the coil method, were usually smooth on the outside, although some were cord marked. Occasionally, pots were decorated with small nodes or indentations, but the majority were plain. The women made both bowls and cooking pots. The pots usually held one or two quarts, but some of the larger ones held as much as two or three gallons.

Crude clay figurines, also found at the sites, may have been used in fertility ceremonies related to agriculture. The figurines usually have a cylindrical body, with a head, nose, and breasts but no arms or legs. Some of the marks on the figurines may represent jewelry, clothing, or tattooing.

Washita focus figurine fragment showing lines that probably represent a necklace and sash. Photo from the Sam Noble Oklahoma Museum of Natural History.

The Plains Village farmers still lived in modest-sized villages of 75 to 150 people. Their settlements were typically placed on terraces of rivers and major streams in western Oklahoma, where fertile soils were located. A village typically might have from 5 to 20 houses and from 75 to 100 inhabitants. The villages were scattered, some miles apart and others within sight of one another. Houses were square or rectangular in floor plan, with walls from 20 to 28 feet long. A framework of wooden posts 5 to 8 inches in diameter formed the support for the walls. The posts were set upright in holes averaging about 10 inches deep and 25 inches apart. The space between the posts was filled with sticks or cane, then the walls were plastered with daub (a mixture of clay and grass). The finished walls were probably 8 to 10 inches thick. Center posts supported a steeply pitched roof of grass thatch whose eaves probably hung well out over the walls to keep the daub from being washed away when it rained. Logs of red cedar, cottonwood, and other trees that were used for the posts must have presented considerable problems in cutting and transportation. The logs may have been floated down the river or hauled to the village.

The Plains Village farmers made tools from a variety of materials. Bone was used for hoes, sickles, digging sticks, flakers, and arrowpoints. Pecked and ground stone was used for milling basins, mortars, hammerstones, celts, and grooved abraders for smoothing arrow shafts or bone tools. Plains Villagers also made a variety of chipped stone arrowpoints, knives, and several kinds of scrapers. Wood was probably used as well, but no wooden tools have survived. There is also limited evidence that the Plains Village farmers used basketry and other woven materials.

The Plains Village farmers buried their dead in cemeteries near their villages. From the study of bones found in the burials, archeologists have learned the size of plains men and women, approximately how old they were at the time of death, and something about their state of health as well as the nature of their burial customs. The people were a little smaller than modern Oklahomans. The men averaged about five feet six inches and the women about five feet one-half inch. While Plains Village farmers lived a harsh, physically demanding life, they were remarkably healthy. Because of an absence of health care for the young, slightly more than half of all deaths occurred between birth and four years of age. There were few deaths among young adults. Although only one third of the population lived beyond age thirty, 17 percent reached the age of fifty or sixty. People suffered from arthritis and a variety of dental problems, including tooth decay. A few died as a result of violence in feuds or raids, but the majority of early deaths were due to disease or complications at birth. The burials were simple. The body was usually placed in a curled-up position with the head facing east. A socially prominent person's burial might include a few grave goods such as a pot or tools that the person had used during life, but these offerings were not elaborate.

The Roy Smith Site

The way of life of the Plains Village farmers of the Oklahoma panhandle was similar to that of their contemporaries in south central Oklahoma, the farmers growing corn and other crops and hunting buffalo, but their houses were unique because of their stone foundations. From A.D. 1250 to A.D. 1450 Plains Village farmers inhabited the Roy Smith site in Beaver County, along the Beaver River in the semiarid high plains region. When a University of Oklahoma field school in archeology excavated the site in 1965, they found that the sandstone slabs forming the walls of the house rested directly on bedrock. The slabs had been pecked into rough rectangles and were held upright by clay packed around the bases. The slabs were no more than three feet high, but in some wall sections another layer may have been added for height.

The western wall of the house ran unbroken for about seventy feet. Along this wall, five areas were sectioned off into rooms averaging fifteen and one-half feet by eleven and one-half feet. There may have been an extended family living in each room. The archeologists also found four post holes in the main room at the southern end of the building, which had been pecked into the hard bedrock floor to hold upright poles. The poles supported crossbeams that probably were covered with tree limbs and thatched with grass to form the roof. This main room was rectangular, running seventeen and one-half feet from east to west and fifteen feet from north to south. A long, narrow entryway in the east wall, about seven feet long and a little more than one and one-half feet wide, led into the room from outside.

Two rooms, which contained large quantities of bone and flint, may have been used to prepare food, make chipped stone tools, and work hides. Three small, circular rooms on the southeast side of the house were probably used to store crops. A bone hoe and knife were found in these storage rooms at the Roy Smith site, and tools associated with farming have sometimes been found in similar circular rooms at other Oklahoma panhandle sites. The Plains Village farmers who lived at the Roy Smith site grew corn and hunted buffalo. They also hunted antelope and ate some fish and mussels. They made cord-marked pottery and used bows and arrows as well as spears.

The Roy Smith house is unusual because its walls were built of stone. The main room, entrance way, and a possible storage room are shown here. Photo from Oklahoma Archeological Survey Files.

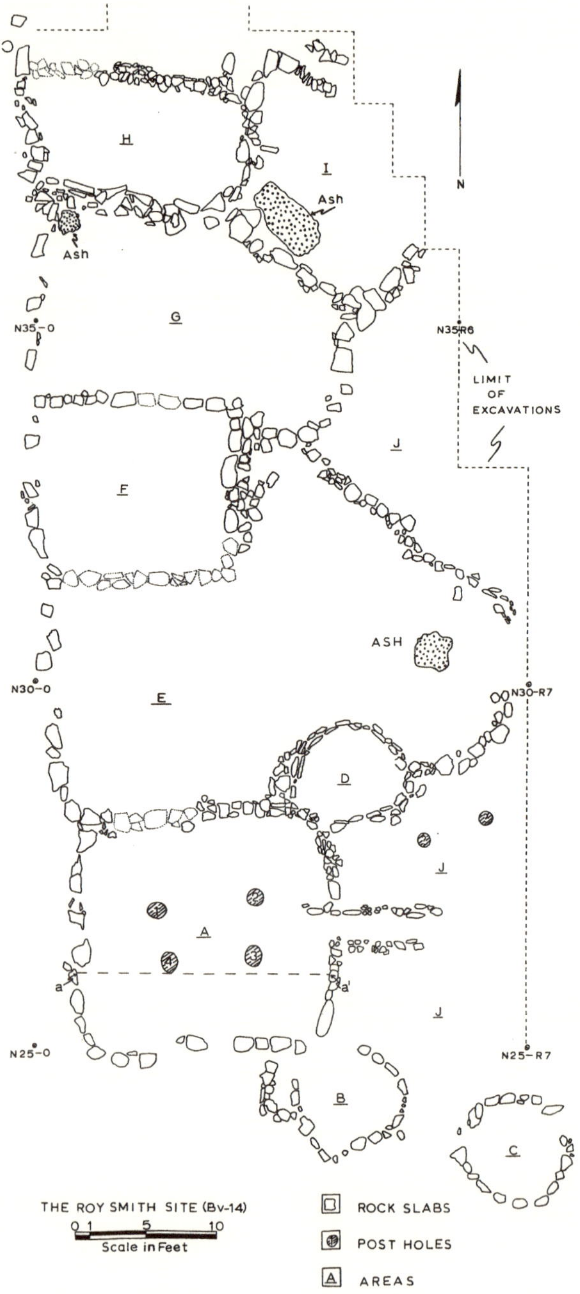

Floor plan of the prehistoric house at the Roy Smith site. Courtesy of the Oklahoma Anthropological Society.

These Plains Villagers were not isolated. Articles found at the Roy Smith site indicate that they traded with other plains and southwestern people. Most of the flaked stone tools found at the site were made of Alibates flint, a red or brown and white flint found in the Texas panhandle about one hundred miles away. Obsidian at the site came from New Mexico. Two small beads made from Pacific Coast shells indicate that the panhandle farmers participated in a trade network that extended all the way from the Pacific Ocean. The contact was not necessarily direct, however. It is possible that the exchange of ideas and goods spread slowly from group to group, the whole system making a network that covered a large part of western North America.

The Plains Village farmers living on the eastern edge of central and western Oklahoma also maintained trading relationships with their neighors in eastern Oklahoma. These groups in eastern Oklahoma, known as the Caddoan cultures, occupied the Arkansas and Red River basins.

5

Caddoan Mound Builders

A.D. 1000 to A.D. 1500

Today the bones of the chief's brother would be carried into the mortuary. The body had already lain in the building until the flesh had fallen away from the skeleton. Now the bones and rich offerings were carried through the temple complex with great ceremony. The boy watched the preparations with excited eyes. He and his family had come from their tiny village some five miles to the west to witness the ceremony.

A young hawk dancer passed by, wearing copper ornaments and a conch-shell pendant necklace. His cape of rabbit-fur yarn fluttered out behind him, showing the hawk-feather design woven into it. The young man joined a group of other men dressed in the hawk regalia, and they slowly began dancing.

Later, the boy saw the cedar-pole litter carried in procession to the temple. It was so large and heaped so high with grave goods that six warriors had to carry it. The boy saw engraved conch-shell cups, copper plates, and freshwater pearls. Heaps of shell beads and blankets covered the bones. At last, as the sunset glowed golden off the treetops, the litter disappeared into the mortuary. The boy and his family went back to their small farm, tired but happy at witnessing the sacred rituals correctly performed. Their leaders were strong, and the people were safe.

Archeological information suggests that scenes such as this were probably familiar at Spiro Mounds in Le Flore County around eight hundred years ago.

The period from A.D. 1000 to A.D. 1400 saw the rise of the Caddoan mound builders in eastern Oklahoma. These people, called "Caddoan" after their language family, were probably the ancestors of the historic Caddo and Wichita confederacies visited by Spanish explorers in the sixteenth century. The Caddoan people of eastern Oklahoma were one of the westernmost groups to share in the Mississippian culture common to many tribes in the southeastern United States. While many of the patterns in Mississippian culture bear resemblances to cultural patterns recognized among Central American societies, archeologists think that the mound-building cultures of the southeast developed their sophisticated mortuary and religious practices independently over a period of some five hundred to one thousand years.

The major centers of Caddoan culture in eastern Oklahoma were within the Arkansas River valley at the Harlan and Norman sites in Wagoner and Cherokee Counties and at the Spiro Mounds in Le Flore County. There were many smaller regional centers such as Reed, Eufaula, Parris, and Hughes Mounds that were also extremely important. Another group of Caddoans occupied the Red River valley in McCurtain, Choctaw, and Pushmataha Counties.

Some archeologists believe that a people who had lived in Louisiana and east Texas migrated to Oklahoma over three thousand years ago and eventually became the Caddoan cultures of the ninth through the fifteenth centuries. These farmers grew corn, beans, squash, sunflowers, tobacco, and a variety of other plants along the Red River. In the Arkansas River valley, they maintained a life-style based on hunting and gathering, with only limited cultivation of corn. The people gathered nettles for making cloth as well as other wild plants for various uses. The labor was probably divided between men and women's work, as it was in historic times. The men hunted, helped to build houses, made war, took leading roles in politics, and broke ground for planting. The women tended the crops after they were planted, kept house, took care of the children, made pottery, and also helped to build houses. Crops were planted on the fertile bottomland. The early farmers used digging tools of bone, wood, and flint that worked well on the rich floodplain soils.

On the basis of accounts of early historic Caddoan society in Arkansas and Louisiana, it is suspected that the people's ancestors were matrilineal, tracing their descent through the female line. Important ancestors in a matrilineal society are the mother, her sister, the grandmother, and so forth. Children are the heirs of their mothers and their mother's brothers. In matrilineal societies, women often have a great deal of power.

The early Caddo constructed houses and temples that were square or rectangular in floor plan, with four

Spiroan farmers were probably women.

center posts supporting the roof. Some later structures had only two center posts, and a few were circular. To begin the building, a row of posts was set upright in the ground. Smaller saplings and/or cane poles were laid vertically between the logs to form the walls. A single entrance, often with an extended doorway, was the only way into the structure. The walls were covered with daub, and the roof was thatched with grass.

The Harlan Site

The Harlan site in Cherokee County is the earliest known major center of Caddoan culture in Oklahoma, although it was established later than similar sites in Texas and Louisiana. Excavations were conducted at the site in 1949, 1950, and 1958, before it was covered by the waters of Fort Gibson Lake. The excavations were directed by Robert E. Bell of the University of Oklahoma.

The Harlan site consisted of one large mound, three smaller mounds, and one compound mound composed of three small, linked mounds. The whole site covered an area of about twenty acres. The main burial mound contained the fragmentary remains of 127 individuals and numerous artifacts. Most of the burials had deteriorated to such an extent that only teeth, long bones of the legs, and portions of skulls remained.

Most of the people were buried lying on their sides in a flexed position. Many of the individuals were disarticulated; the bones had been cleaned and the skeleton placed in position before the burial. The artifacts found were generally grave goods included with the burials. Such objects in the upper-class burials were often luxury items, whereas those in a common person's burial were domestic objects. The inclusion of grave goods was a means of showing concern and respect for the dead as well as showing the status of the individuals making the offerings.

Grave goods found at the Harlan site include items such as arrowpoints, spearpoints, and stone knives; engraved pottery vessels; beads of shell, stone, and wood; beads and earspools (a type of earrings) covered with a thin veneer of copper; stone pipes; cane matting;

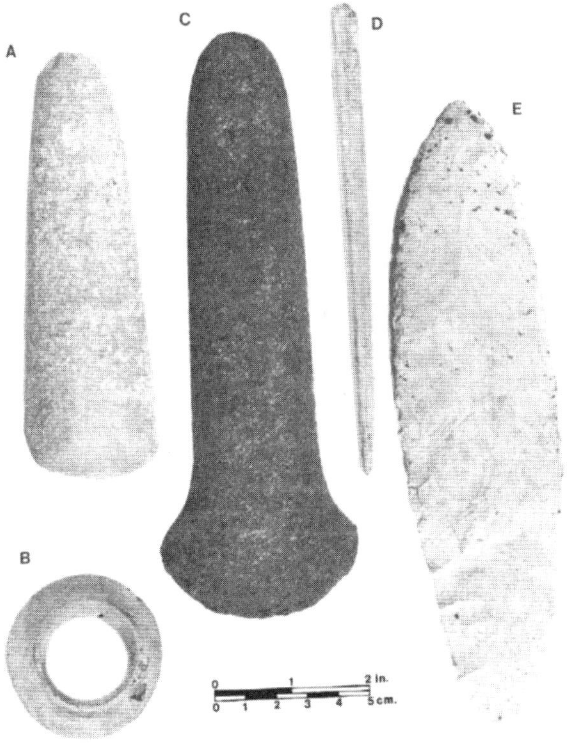

Artifacts are from the Harlan site in Cherokee County: (a) celt, (b) earspool, (c) stone spud, (d) bone awl, (e) knife. Photos courtesy of the Oklahoma Anthropological Society.

and a long-nosed god maskette of copper. This maskette was small, about the size of the palm of a hand, and was probably worn as part of a headdress. Archeologists also found a stone mace as well as stone and shell hoe blades. Organic stains in the soil indicated that there may have been other grave goods, such as wooden artifacts and woven material that were not preserved.

The excavators found little evidence of people living near the mounds. Instead, the site apparently served as a mortuary and religious center for the scattered farming communities located along the Grand River valley and Fourteen Mile Creek. The site dates from about A.D. 700 to A.D. 1400, but its heaviest period of use was from A.D. 900 to A.D. 1200. The priests or some other caretakers probably lived in the few houses discovered on the site. The earlier burials had few grave goods,

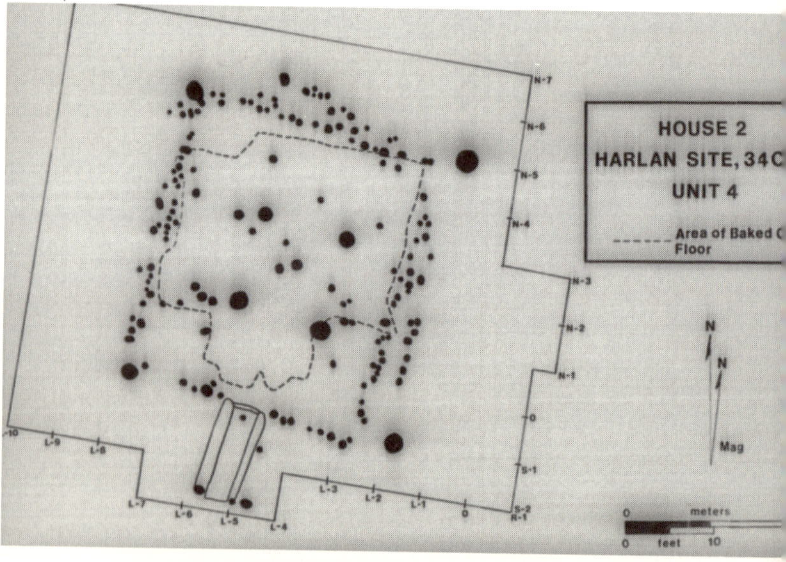

The pattern of postholes from this house at the Harlan site helps archeologists understand how the Caddoan people built their houses. Courtesy of the Oklahoma Anthropological Society.

and these burials were usually of a simple type. Later burials became increasingly elaborate. After A.D. 1200 the Harlan site began to lose some of its prominence, and this elaboration of religious ceremony reached its peak at the Spiro Mounds site, some ninety miles downstream.

The Spiro Mounds

The most famous Caddoan site in Oklahoma is the Spiro Mounds site in Le Flore County. It is known not only for the extraordinary, well-preserved artifacts recovered there, but also for the controversy that surrounded its first excavations. The local inhabitants knew about the mounds for nearly one hundred years before they received any attention from the scientific community. Most people living near the site in the 1930s were descendants of Choctaws and their freed slaves who had

T-shaped stone pipe from the Spiro Mounds site (not to scale). Photo from the Sam Noble Oklahoma Museum of Natural History.

received land allotments after the Civil War. They were familiar with the mounds found in other parts of the southeastern United States, so they knew that the Spiro Mounds contained burials. Because this made them sacred ground, they were left unmolested until commercial diggers began work on the site in the 1930s. The work culminated with the mining of Spiro by unemployed coal miners in the early 1930s.

From 1933 to 1935 the so-called "Pocola Mining Company," which held a lease on the site, dug into the mounds and carried away numerous artifacts that were sold at high prices in East Coast markets. Carl Guthe, then chairman of the National Research Council Committee on State Archeological Surveys, contacted Forrest E. Clements of the University of Oklahoma Department of Anthropology for more information

This drawing is based on a photograph of Craig Mound taken by James Thoburn in December 1913. Original photo from the Sam Noble Oklahoma Museum of Natural History.

about the site. Clements went to see the mounds and met the group of men who called themselves the "Pocola Mining Company."

After prolonged, difficult negotiations, Clements obtained a lease on the site for the University of Oklahoma that was scheduled to begin as soon as the mining company's lease expired. Clements then went to California for the summer. He returned to find that the miners had continued their work despite the new state law that prohibited digging in archeological sites without a license. He later recalled:

> I shall never forget the shock and grief I experienced when, upon my return in the late fall, I learned that the digging had been resumed during the summer and had been allowed to proceed unmolested; that the great mound had been tunneled through and through, gutted in a frenzy of haste. I went to look at it. Sections of cedar poles lay scattered on the ground, fragments of feather and fur textiles littered the whole area; it was impossible to take a single step in hundreds of square yards around the ruined structure without scuffing up broken pieces of pottery, sections of engraved shell, and beads of shell, stone, and bone. The site was abandoned; the diggers had completed their work. (Clements 1945:56)

Despite this tragic looting of the mound, scientific excavation began in 1936 and continued through the 1941 season under Clement's overall direction. During the 1960s, Don Wyckoff, Oklahoma State Archeologist, located additional mounds at the site. Limited excavations were conducted in the 1970s at the Craig Mound. Due to a lack of funds, however, major excavations were not renewed at the site until 1979. During the 1979 season, J. Daniel Rogers of the Oklahoma Archeological Survey conducted excavations at the Spiro Mounds site with funds provided by the Oklahoma Department of Parks and Tourism and the U.S. Heritage Conservation and Recreation Service.

The mounds at Spiro have yielded a tremendous amount and variety of information and artifacts. The site consists of at least twelve mounds covering an area of approximately eighty acres. The main features of the site are two groups of mounds: Craig Mound, which contained the Great Mortuary and the two Ward Mounds, and Brown and Copple mounds, along with the other small mounds that cover the remains of buildings.

Members of the Pocola Mining Company at Craig Mound. The company held the lease on the Spiro Mounds site from 1933 until 1935. Photo from the Sam Noble Oklahoma Museum of Natural History.

The rulers of the Spiro site achieved their dominance over the surrounding area because of the site's key position on the Arkansas River. Originally, there was a village on the site, as well as what are now called Brown Mound and Copple Mound. The Spiro elite controlled a large area downstream and to the north and south of the site. Their position on the Arkansas River allowed them to manipulate trade between the Plains Village farmers to the west and the other major cultural centers in the southeastern United States. They probably exercised military control, since many of the ceremonial

Craig Mound being excavated under the supervision of University of Oklahoma archeologists. The university obtained the lease in 1935. Photo from the Sam Noble Oklahoma Museum of Natural History.

During the summer of 1979, students from the University of Oklahoma field school and high-school students from the Archeology in Action program participated in further excavations at the Spiro Mounds. Photo from Oklahoma Archeological Survey Files.

objects found were weapons or weapon-derived forms. Gradually, Spiro grew into a major religious center with only a few caretakers actually living at the site. The village was abandoned, and the Great Mortuary was built. This period of major religious importance occurred between A.D. 1350 and A.D. 1450.

The Spiro elite were part of what archeologists call a *chiefdom.* In a chiefdom the highest ranking person has control over critical resources. At Spiro this meant control over trade in luxury goods and the products of local farmers, as well as military leadership. Everyone is related to everyone else in a chiefdom, with rank within the group depending upon how closely one is related to the chief. At Spiro high rank meant special treatment even in death.

The Mounds

The mounds at the Spiro site were important in the assignment of rank. Many regional ceremonial centers, as well as local cemeteries, were scattered throughout the area under the Spiroan chiefdom's control. Burials in local cemeteries, which usually contained only a few utilitarian grave goods, were outranked in status by burials in regional centers containing some luxury goods. These, in turn, had lower status than the spectacular display of grave goods at Spiro.

Not all Caddoan mounds were the same; there were three types of these earth constructions. One type of mound was raised as a platform for a structure. Such mounds were usually in the shape of a truncated pyramid, with a ramp on at least one side. The second type was an earthen cover over a destroyed building, generally ranging in size from 2.5 feet high and 40 feet in diameter to 3.5 feet high and 75 feet in diameter. The third type was an accretional burial mound, built up of increasing layers of burials, burial goods, and earth. The Spiro site contained all three types of mounds as well as combinations of the types, as can be found at Craig Mound.

The Great Mortuary

The Great Mortuary was found at the base of the main cone in Craig Mound. It was built on the remains of a still earlier mortuary and covered an area of some

Some rare pieces of polychrome cloth from the Spiro Mounds site (variable scale). Photos by J. Tribble, Sam Noble Oklahoma Museum of Natural History.

fifty-five by thirty-seven feet. The elite Spiroan dead decomposed at the Great Mortuary before their final interment in an accretional burial mound.

Within the Great Mortuary there were at least three classes of burials. The very highest ranking were the litter burials. Cedar pole litters, ranging in size from six by seven feet to two by two feet, were heaped with luxury goods and the bones of the honored dead. In the second class of burials, the bones were laid out in an extended position and surrounded by a few artifacts. The lowest or third-class burials were bundles of bones placed in woven baskets that contained limited numbers of offerings. It is possible that cremations were also a form of burial, but by their nature they leave little trace.

Conch shell found with individual in Brown Mound. Photo from the Sam Noble Oklahoma Museum of Natural History.

A large crematory basin measuring sixteen feet in diameter was found at the base of the second mound unit. The basin was about 1.6 feet deep, with three sets of steps leading down into it. This basin was not in the Great Mortuary and probably relates to an earlier period of ceremonialism at Spiro.

Drawing of a design found on an engraved shell cup from Craig Mound. From Philip Phillips and James A. Brown, *Pre-Columbian Shell Engravings from the Craig Mound at Spiro, Oklahoma,* Paperback Edition Part 1. Peabody Museum Press. Copyright 1978 by the President and Fellows of Harvard College.

Drawing of a design found on an engraved shell cup from Craig Mound. From Philip Phillips and James A. Brown, *Pre-Columbian Shell Engravings from the Craig Mound at Spiro, Oklahoma,* Paperback Edition Part 1. Peabody Museum Press. Copyright 1978 by the President and Fellows of Harvard College.

The Central Chamber

One of the great mysteries of Spiro has been the nature of the Central Chamber. When members of the "Pocola Mining Company" tunneled into the center of the main cone, they reached the remains of the Great Mortuary. There were many tales spread at that time about an elaborate central chamber at the heart of the mound. The stories of this chamber are fascinating and sometimes conflicting.

During his excavations in the 1930s, Clements made observations and measurements in an attempt to find out whether the story was true. First, he examined the interior of the mound where the relic miners had been working. Toward the end of the lease period, the miners broke into three mutually distrustful factions, and this may have been the reason why three tunnels were driven into the mound from different directions to meet in a hollowed space in the center. Clements said:

> This chamber was irregular, varying from fifteen to twenty feet across and was perhaps eight feet from the floor to the center of the roof. There was no indication that it was of other than recent excavation, for tool marks were thick over its claylike walls. It was bare

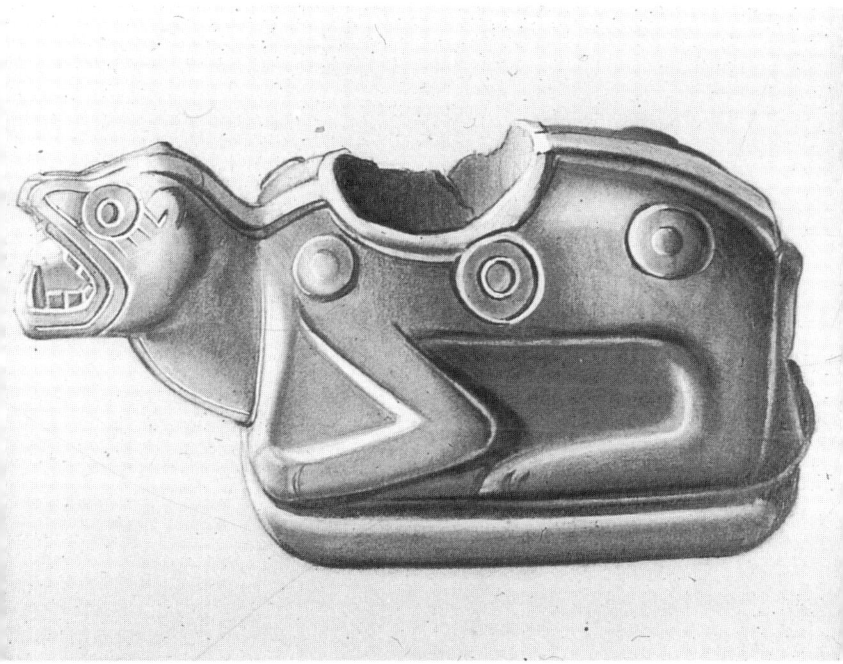

Stone pipe from the Spiro Mounds site, resting warrior figure (not to scale). Photo from the Sam Noble Oklahoma Museum of Natural History.

except for a few gin bottles and cigarette stubs. The great cone, therefore, was but a thick shell of earth. (Clements 1945:61)

Next, Clements examined the amount of earth removed from the mound by the miners. They had taken the earth removed from tunneling the main cone and wheeled it in barrows to a nearby dump. All of the loose earth was sifted through screens during the W.P.A. work on the site. The total amount was esti-

Drawing of design found on an engraved shell cup from Craig Mound. From Philip Phillips and James A. Brown, *Pre-Columbian Shell Engravings from Craig Mound at Spiro, Oklahoma,* Paperback Edition Part 1. Peabody Museum Press. Copyright 1978 by the President and Fellows of Harvard College.

mated at six thousand cubic feet. The three tunnels, according to Clements's estimate, would account for about one thousand cubic feet. Since all the dirt came from the interior of the mound, the remaining five thousand cubic feet must have come from a chamber hollowed out by the miners themselves.

James Brown of Northwestern University has reexamined Clements's calculations and found some exceptions, however. Based on the presence of a calcium-hardened wall and the excellent preservation of perishable artifacts in the central chamber, Brown argues convincingly for the presence of such a burial vault. This structure would have covered an area some fifteen feet in diameter, with cedar posts set an angle to form a dome over the chamber's floor. Rather than burials being placed in this area over time, apparently burials extending over four hundred years of Spiro's occupation were unearthed and placed in the central chamber at one time, symbolizing closure of this important period for the religious leaders at Spiro. After the event, a cap of dirt was placed over the cedar posts to form the cone of Craig Mound.

Caddoan Religion

The grave goods found at Spiro fall into three broad classes: weapons and weapon-related objects such as monolithic stone axes and maces; ritual objects such as copper hawk-dancer plates and long-nosed-god effigy masks; and perishable items such as baskets, clothing, wood, and shell. They all display a highly developed artistic skill and tradition, and the majority of the decoration has a religious theme or symbolism. The most spectacular object is the engraved conch shell found in the Craig Mound. In all, over 2,200 complete and fragmentary shells were recovered.

The engravings, which depict Spiro social life as well as more symbolic religious subjects, represent one of the most complete depictions of a prehistoric culture unearthed in North America. Most of what we know about early Caddoan religion comes from such grave goods. Despite these portrayals, all we can say with certainty regarding the Caddoan religion is that elaborate burial of the elite dead was a major feature of the culture, and that many of the artistic motifs were like motifs used by people in similar cultural centers in other parts of the southeastern United States. We would prefer a detailed account, but the people at Spiro, despite the complexity of their culture, did not have a written language. This means that archeologists must obtain their knowledge from the ritual objects and the archaeological context that have survived the passage of time and the dangers of nonscientific excavation.

Some archeologists have analyzed Caddoan religious art motifs, especially those found on engraved shell cups and gorgets (a type of pendants). They have concluded that the Caddoan religion was part of what is called the Southern Cult, named after the many traits certain southeastern sites have in common. Presently, there are two possible interpretations of these designs: the people may have believed in a single god with many attributes, they may have believed in a number of gods, the serpent and falcon representing the two main gods.

A dancing human figure dressed in a falcon costume was a frequently used design in Spiroan and other southeastern art. Serpents and, possibly, people in serpent costume were often depicted. Other animals, especially

Three of the copper hawk dancer plates from the Spiro Mounds site (variable scale). The Spiroan people had no gold or silver, and copper was their most precious metal. Photo by J. Tribble, Sam Noble Oklahoma Museum of Natural History.

spiders and human beings engaged in ceremonial activity, were also engraved on shell.

Gradual Decline

During late Caddoan times, a new sun and fire symbolism rose to greater prominence. Spanish explorers found sun worship common among the Caddo confederacies of northern Texas in the sixteenth century. We cannot be certain as to exactly what happened, but we do know that mound building gradually ceased between A.D. 1400 and A.D. 1500. The main portion of Craig

Monolithic stone ax from the Spiro Mounds site (not to scale). Photo from the Sam Noble Oklahoma Museum of Natural History.

Mound was finished with a conical cap of earth, and no more burials or mortuary building took place there. There seems to have been a conscious, deliberate decision to stop using the site. The mound cap was neatly finished, and there were no signs of war or violence.

The people of eastern Oklahoma continued farming,

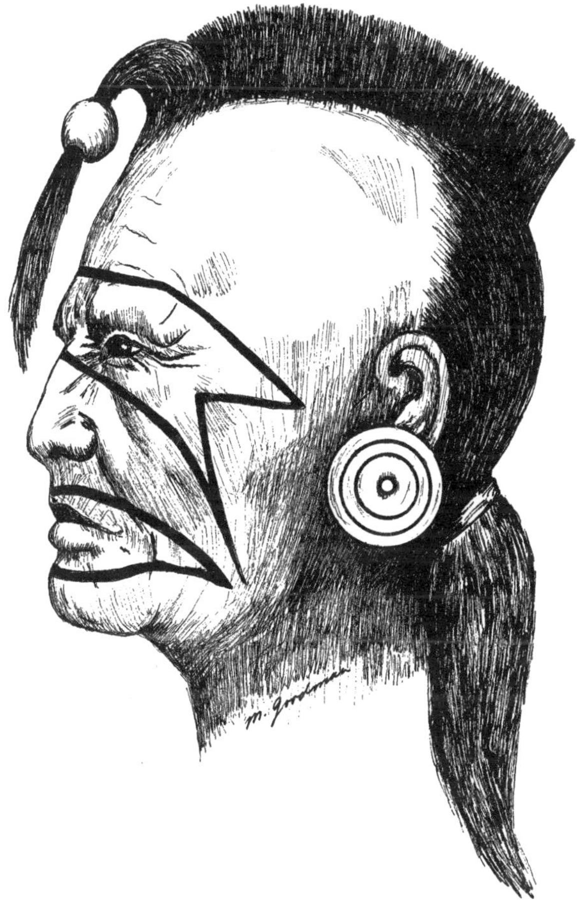

The earspools had a pulley-shaped back that fit into enlarged holes in the earlobe.

with more emphasis on the growing of corn, and hunting buffalo. They also began to trade more frequently with people to the west, rather than with people to the east as they had during the Spiro elites' ascendancy. The elite themselves seem to have disappeared. Whether this was due to disease, decline in birth rate, or another cause cannot be determined. The elaborate burials ceased with the end of the mound building. Between A.D. 1500 and A.D. 1700, drier conditions on the southern plains led to an expansion of the buffalo range, and this, in turn, led to a dramatic increase in buffalo hunting.

a

b

c

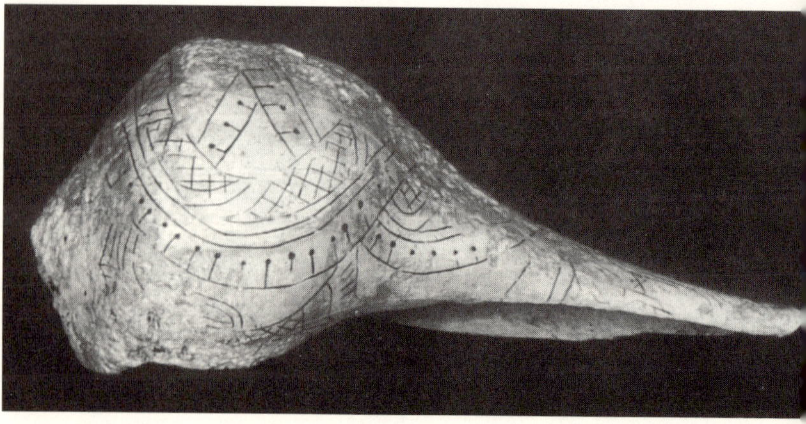

d

Artifacts from the Spiro Mounds site: (a) shell gorget, (b) stone earspool, (c) carved shell pendant, (d) clay jar, (e) clay bowl (variable scale). Photos from the Sam Noble Oklahoma Museum of Natural History.

e

6

Early Historic Buffalo Hunters

A.D. 1500 to A.D. 1700

They circled on foot, the whole tribe moving slowly through the grass, driving the buffalo inexorably towards the compound. There were only fifty members in the tribe and about two hundred animals in the herd. The hunters edged in and out of view of the buffalo, careful not to scare them into an early stampede. The young man behind the pile of rocks waited patiently. As the herd moved into view, he glimpsed his sister among the drivers. The buffalo bunched together as they were driven by the tightening funnel of humans. The corral was just ahead, the drop-off invisible to the oncoming herd.

Suddenly, all the encircling hunters emerged. The buffalo started uneasily, trotting forward. At a signal from the hunt leader, the young man sprang forward from behind the concealing pile of stones. Yelling, the others hiding behind nearby piles also emerged. The herd broke into a run. The hunters raced back and forth, forming a human fence and forcing the buffalo into the trap. The herd stampeded over the edge and into the corral. Once they were inside, there was no way out. The hunters quickly killed the panicking, milling animals, and the butchering began.

Life in a historic Wichita village such as Deer Creek in Kay County would have been much like this during the buffalo hunts.

After A.D. 1500 the climate in western Oklahoma became too dry for dependable farming, and the people increasingly turned to buffalo as their chief source of food. The buffalo hunters generally used a combination of the drive and the surround. This group effort required strict discipline of the hunters, as the welfare of the whole tribe depended upon the success of the hunt. The people also hunted deer, antelope, and rabbits, generally using bows and arrows. They also gathered wild plant foods and planted small crops of corn when there was enough water.

The buffalo hunters abandoned their more permanent houses and lived in grass dwellings and tipis. The conical tents with covers of buffalo hide were easily put up and taken down. People followed the herds on foot, as horses did not reach Oklahoma until they were reintroduced by the Spanish around A.D. 1700.

People living in the slightly wetter climate of eastern Oklahoma continued farming but made increasing use of buffalo. Archeologists have found larger amounts of bison-bone tools and debris in sites from this period. The eastern farmers made periodic hunting expeditions into the western plains seeking buffalo, then returned to their villages.

In prehistoric and early historic times buffalo herds

wandered at will, seeking the best water and forage. They had no invariable annual north-south migration patterns, and so the hunters followed their erratic movements closely. This nomadic life-style meant that, as in the time of the foragers, possessions had to be light and easily transportable. The early buffalo hunters used domesticated dogs as pack animals. A member of the Coronado expedition in the 1540s wrote:

> They travel like the Arabs with their tents and troops of dogs loaded with poles and having Moorish pack saddles

Buffalo herd at rest on Wells Flat in the Wichita Mountains National Wildlife Refuge. Western History Collections, University of Oklahoma Libraries.

and girths. When the load gets disarranged, the dogs howl, calling someone to fix them right.

WINSHIP (translator) 1896:527

These saddle-and-pole arrangements came to be called travois.

Buffalo provided meat, hide clothing and shelter, and bone tools. The animals undoubtedly played a major role in the religious and social organization of the hunters, as we know they did a few generations later, based on descriptions of historic tribes. The hunters' methods of preparing the buffalo were not the same as those used today, but made full use of the resources at hand. From the account of the Coronado expedition we learn that:

This drawing is based upon an early illustration of an American buffalo that appeared in Andre Thevet's *Les Singularitez de la France Anarcique,* Antwerp, 1558.

These people eat raw flesh and drink blood. . . . They dry the flesh [of the buffalo] in the sun, cutting it thin like a leaf, and when dry they grind it like meal and make a sort of sea soup of it to eat. A handful thrown into a pot swells so as to increase very much. They season it with fat. . . . They empty the large gut and fill it with blood, and carry this around the neck to drink when they are thirsty. When they open the belly of a cow [buffalo], they squeeze out the chewed grass and drink the juice that remains behind. because they say this contains the essence of the stomach.

Winship (translator) 1896:527-28

These artifacts from the Edwards site in Beckham County show some of the beads, arrowpoints, and fragments of pottery used by early buffalo hunters. Photo from Oklahoma Archeological Survey Files.

European settlers called the dried meat "pemmican." Native Americans often flavored pemmican with fruit or berries to improve its taste. It kept indefinitely without spoiling and weighed only about two-thirds as much as the same amount of fresh meat, both important considerations in the days before canning and easy transportation.

The Native American cultures had by this time diversified into a number of tribes and confederacies having different customs, beliefs, and languages. The plains tribes, communicated with one another by means of sign language. Some of the plains hunters were Apache Indians. There were several different groups among the Apache, but historians include them all under the term "Plains Apache." Other tribes may have been ancestors of the modern Kiowa and Wichita bands such as the Ouasitas, Taovayas, Tawakonis, and Iscanis.

The European explorers and settlers brought horses with them to the New World. Many of these horses were lost or stolen, and around A.D. 1700, they started appearing in Oklahoma. The acquisition of horses made buffalo hunting much easier, and many tribes who had heretofore primarily been farmers moved onto the plains around this time. Other tribes moved westward because of the pressure from increasingly large European settlements.

The two centuries that followed were full of turmoil and change. Buffalo were hunted nearly to extinction, and several tribes that had existed before historic times died out or were diminished. The tribes fought the Euroamerican settlers and, even more disastrously, fought among themselves, so that they were never able to unite in an effective resistance. The story of these turbulent years marks the beginning of United States history and the end of this chronicle of Oklahoma's prehistoric people.

THE DUNCAN SITE

Because of the nomadic way of life and the impermanent dwellings of the historic buffalo hunters, archeologists have found less evidence of their camps and villages than they have found for earlier groups. The shorter time span of this period (three hundred years) also limits the number of sites that exist and might possibly be found. One site that was reported and has

Field investigations at the protohistoric Duncan site in Washita County. Photo from Oklahoma Archeological Survey Files.

been studied is the Duncan site in Washita County. The location of the site had been known to artifact collectors in western Oklahoma since archeologist Harold Brighton recorded it in 1951. In 1981 archaeologists Tim Baugh and Richard Drass conducted limited excavations at Duncan. They followed this work with University of Oklahoma/Archeological Survey-sponsored field-school excavations in 1983.

Pit containing broken bison bone. Bison bones were probably being shattered for extraction of marrow for bone grease. Photo from Oklahoma Archeological Survey Files.

These investigations provided valuable insights into the lives of people living in western Oklahoma roughly 650 to 400 years ago. The excavations led to the recovery of large quantities of buffalo bone, much of which had been shattered to remove the marrow and make bone grease. Artifacts found at the Duncan site include obsidian, turquoise, painted ceramics, and marine shells from the coastal area of southern California. These goods point to a thriving trade with pueblos in eastern New Mexico such as Picuris and Pecos. The pueblos may also have traded corn to the people living at the Duncan

site, because while corn was found there, there were few tools such as hoes that would be used for agriculture.

One of the most intriguing finds at the Duncan site was the evidence of a palisade that would have enclosed a 1.3-acre area within the village. There do not appear to have been any houses inside this enclosure. The Duncan site is too early for the enclosure to have been a corral for horses. Archeologists continue to study this feature in the hopes of understanding whether it was built for protection of the site's inhabitants or for some other purpose.

Reconstruction of a palisade that had been constructed around the Duncan site in protohistoric times. Photo from Oklahoma Archeological Survey Files.

Epilogue

This book offers a brief overview of Oklahoma's dynamic and enduring Native American heritage. Throughout the state, archeologists have recorded over sixteen thousand sites where prehistoric and early historic Native American people camped, killed and butchered game, quarried stone for tools, and created visual images of their world. Archeologists have reconstructed the lifeways of prehistoric cultures from an incredibly fragile record of the past; however, they are at a major crossroads in their study of this record. Technological advances have pushed archeology from the romantic endeavor of archeologists pitted against a land that reluctantly gives up its secrets to a cutting-edge science using techniques such as ground-penetrating radar, computer-graphic information systems, and sophisticated chemical tests. Using these scientific breakthroughs, contemporary archeologists are pitted in a race against time to save a diminishing cultural heritage.

Natural processes such as erosion increasingly contribute to the loss of archeological sites, as does economic development with its accompanying oil and gas wells, gas pipelines, and industrial plants. The most dismaying loss of Oklahoma's cultural heritage, though, comes from commercial looters. Today's commercial pothunters, unlike the unemployed coal miners who destroyed so much at Spiro Mounds, are frequently members of larger crime/drug cartels that have found the artifact market a lucrative area for profit. These are challenges that archeologists must face in order to preserve the past for future generations. Their work also requires the support of the citizens of Oklahoma in reporting archeological finds, combating vandalism, and expanding the treatment of prehistory in the education system.

Bibliography

Anderson, Adrian D.

1975 The Cooperton Mammoth: An Early Man Bone Quarry. *Great Plains Journal* 14 (2):130–75.

Bastian, Tyler

1969 *The Hudsonpillar and Freeman Sites, North Central Oklahoma*. Archeological Site Report 14.

Oklahoma River Basin Survey and University of Oklahoma Research Institute, Norman.

Bell, Robert E.

1972 *The Harlan Site, Ck-6, A Prehistoric Mound Center in Cherokee County, Eastern Oklahoma.* Oklahoma Anthropological Society Memoir 2, Oklahoma City.

1984 The Plains Villagers: The Washita River. In *Prehistory of Oklahoma,* edited by Robert E. Bell, 307–24. Orlando: Academic Press.

Bell, Robert E., ed.

1984 *Prehistory of Oklahoma.* New York: Academic Press.

Bement, Leland C.

1999 *Bison Hunting at Cooper Site: Where Lightening Bolts Drew Thundering Herds.* Norman: University of Oklahoma Press.

Briscoe, James

1977 *The Plantation Site (Mi-63), An Early Caddoan Settlement in Eastern Oklahoma.* Papers in Highway Archaeology 3. Oklahoma Highway Archaeological Survey, Oklahoma City.

Brooks, Robert L.

1987 *The Arthur Site: Settlement and Subsistence Structure at a Washita River Phase Village.* Oklahoma Archeological Survey, Studies in Oklahoma's Past 15.

Brown, James A.

1966 *Spiro Studies, Volume 1: Description of the Mound Group.* First Part of the Second Annual Report on Caddoan Archeology, Spiro Focus Research, Stovall Museum of Science and History and the University of Oklahoma Research Institute, Norman.

1973 Spiro Art and its Mortuary Contexts. In *Death and the Afterlife in PreColumbian America,* Dumbarton Oaks Research Library and Collections, edited by Elizabeth P. Benson, Washington, D.C.

1996 *The Spiro Ceremonial Center: The Archaeology of Arkansas Valley Caddoan Culture in Eastern Oklahoma.* 2 vols. Memoir 29. Museum of Anthropology, University of Michigan, Ann Arbor.

Cartledge, Thomas R.

1970 *The Tyler-Rose Site and Late Prehistory in East-Central Oklahoma.* Archaeological Site Report 19. Oklahoma River Basin Survey, University of Oklahoma Research Institute, Norman.

Clements, Forrest E.

1945 Historical Sketch of the Spiro Mound. In The Spiro Mound Collection from the Museum, *Contributions from the Museum of the American Indian,* Heye Foundation 14, New York.

Davis, Hester A.

1969 *What Is Archeology?* In Arkansas Archeological Survey Popular Series 1, Fayetteville.

Dillehay, Tom D., and David J. Meltzer, eds.

1991 *The First Americans: Search and Research.* Boca Raton: CRC Press.

Drass, Richard R.

1997 *Culture Change on the Eastern Margins of the Southern Plains.* Oklahoma Anthropological Society Memoir 7.

Duffield, Lathel Flay

1964 *Engraved Shells from the Craig Mound at Spiro,*

LeFlore County, Oklahoma. Oklahoma Anthropological Society Memoir 1, Oklahoma City.

The Oklahoma Craig Mound: Another Look at an Old Problem. *Bulletin of the Oklahoma Anthropological Society* 22:1–10.

Duncan, Marjorie

1995 Calf Creek Foragers: Mobility on the Southern Plains During the Altithermal. *Bulletin of the Oklahoma Anthropological Society* 42:89–144.

Eddy, Frank W.

1964 *Metates and Manos: The Basic Corn Grinding Tools of the Southwest.* Museum of New Mexico Press, Popular Series Pamphlet 1, Santa Fe.

Frison, George

1970 The Glenrock Buffalo Jump. *Plains Anthropologist* 7, part 2: 15–50.

1991 *Prehistoric Hunters of the High Plains.* New York: Academic Press.

Galm, Jerry

1981 *Prehistoric Cultural Adaptations in the Wister Valley,* Ph.D. diss., Washington State University.

Gilbert, Claudette Marie

1979 *Mammoth Hunters: The Domebo Site.* Prehistoric People of Oklahoma 4, University of Oklahoma Stovall Museum of Science and History and Oklahoma Archeological Survey, Norman.

Griffith, William Joyce

1954 The Hasinai Indians of East Texas as seen by Europeans, 1687–1772. *Philological and Documentary Studies* 1, no. 3, Middle American Research Institute, Tulane University, New Orleans.

Hammatt, Hallett H.

1976 The Gore Pit Site: An Archaic Occupation in Southwestern Oklahoma and a Review of the Archaic Stage in the Southern Plains. *Plains Anthropologist* 1976 (2174), Lincoln, Nebraska.

Hartley, John D.

1974 The Von Elm Site: An Early Plains-Woodland Complex in North Central Oklahoma. *Archaeological Site Report* 28,Oklahoma River Basin Survey and University of Oklahoma Office of Research Administration, Norman.

1977 Archaeological Investigations at the Bryson-Paddock Site: An Early Contact Period Site on the Southern Plains. *Archeological Site Report* 32, Oklahoma River Basin Survey, Norman.

Hester, James J., with sections by Ernest L. Lundelius, Jr., and Ronald Fryxell

1972 Blackwater Locality No. 1: A Stratified Early Man Site in Eastern New Mexico. *Fort Burgwin Research Center Publication* 8, Southern Methodist University, Ranchos de Taos, New Mexico.

Hester, Thomas

1974 Great Basin Atlatl Studies. Ballena Press Publications in *Archeology, Ethnology, and History* 2, edited by Robert F. Heizer, Ramona, California.

Hofman, Jack L.

1978 An Analysis of Surface Material from the Little Deer Site, 34Cu10, of Western Oklahoma: A Further Investigation of the Wheeler Complex. *Bulletin of the Oklahoma Anthropological Society* 27, 1–110. Oklahoma City.

Hofman, Jack L., Robert L. Brooks, Joe S. Hays, Douglas W. Owsley, Richard L. Jantz, Murray K. Marks, and Mary H. Manhein

1989 *From Clovis to Comanchero: Archeological Overview of the Southern Great Plains.* Arkansas Archeological Survey, Research Series 35.

Holmes, Mary Anne

1973 The Packard Site. *Prehistoric People of Oklahoma* 1, University of Oklahoma Stovall Museum and Oklahoma Archeological Survey, Norman.

Holmes, Mary Anne, and Claudette Marie Gilbert

1979 Prehistoric Panhandle Farmers: The Roy Smith Site I Survey and *People of Oklahoma* 3, Oklahoma Archeological Survey and University of Oklahoma Stovall Museum of Science and History, Norman.

Hudson, Charles

1976 *The Southeastern Indians.* Knoxville: University of Tennessee Press.

John, Elizabeth

1975 *Storms Brewed in Other Men's Worlds.* College Station: Texas A&M University Press.

Johnson, Alfred E., ed.

1976 Hopewellian Archaeology in the Lower Missouri Valley. University of Kansas *Publications in Anthropology* 8, Lawrence.

Leonhardy, Frank C., ed.

1961 Domebo: A PaleoIndian Mammoth Kill in the Prairie Plains. *Contributions of the Museum of the Great Plains* 1, Lawton, Oklahoma.

Lewis, Thomas M. N., and Madeline Kneberg

1958 *Tribes That Slumber* Knoxville: University of Tennessee Press.

Lintz, Christopher R.

1986 *Architecture and Community Variability Within the Antelope Creek Phase of the Texas Panhandle.* Oklahoma Archeological Survey, Studies in Oklahoma's Past 14.

McGimsey, Charles R.

1969 Indians of Arkansas. In *Arkansas Archeological Survey Popular Series* 1, Fayetteville.

McHugh, Tom

1972 *The Time of the Buffalo.* New York: Alfred A. Knopf.

Muto, Guy R., with appendices by John D. Northcutt and Don G. Wyckoff

1978 The Habiukut of Eastern Oklahoma, Parris Mound, Part 1, Phase 1. Oklahoma Historical Society *Series in Anthropology* 3, Oklahoma City.

Newcomb, W. W., Jr.

1961 *The Indians of Texas: From Prehistoric to Modem Times.* Austin: University of Texas Press.

Orr, Kenneth G.

1942 *The Eufaula Mound, Oklahoma: Contributions to the Spiro Focus.* Master's thesis, University of Chicago.

Phillips, Philip, and James A. Brown

1978 *Pre-Columbian Shell Engravings from the Craig Mound at Spiro, Oklahoma,* Paperback Edition Part 1. Cambridge, Mass.: Peabody Museum Press, Harvard College, 1978.

Pillaert, E. Elizabeth

1963 The McLemore Site of the Washita River Focus. *Bulletin of the Oklahoma Anthropological Society* 1:1–113, Oklahoma City.

Reynolds, John D.

1979 The Grasshopper Falls Phase of the Plains Woodland. Kansas State Historical Society *Anthropological Series* 7, Topeka.

Rogers, J. Daniel, Don G. Wyckoff, and Dennis A. Peterson, eds.

1989 *Contributions to Spiro Archeology: Mound Excavations and Regional Perspectives.* Oklahoma Archeological Survey, Studies in Oklahoma's Past 16.

Schneider, Fred

1969 The Roy Smith Site, Bv-14., Beaver County, Oklahoma. *Bulletin of the Oklahoma Anthropological Society* 18:110–79.

Schoenwetter, James

1965 How Old Is It? The Story of Dating in Archeology. Museum of New Mexico Press *Popular Series Pamphlet* 2, Santa Fe.

Scientific American

1951 *Early Man in America. Readings from* Scientific American. San Francisco: W. H. Freeman.

Story, Dee Ann

1972 *Preliminary Report of 1968, 1969, and 1970 Excavations at the George C. Davis Site, Cherokee County, Texas.* Report of Field Research Conducted under NSF (GS2573 and 3200) and Interagency Contracts between the University of Texas at Austin and the Texas Building Commission and Texas Historical Survey Committee, Texas.

Story, Dee Ann, and S. Valastro, Jr.

1977 Radiocarbon Dating and the George C. Davis Site, Texas. *Journal of Field Archeology* 4, no. 1, 63–90, Association for Field Archeology, Boston.

Watson, Virginia

1950 The Optima Focus of the Panhandle Aspect: Description and Analysis. *Texas Archaeological Society*

Bulletin 21:7–68. Webb, Clarence H., and Hiram F. Gregory

1978 The Caddo Indians of Louisiana. Department of Culture, Recreation, and Tourism, Louisiana Archaeological Survey and Antiquities Commission *Anthropological Study* 2, Baton Rouge.

Wheat, Joe Ben

1972 The Olsen-Chubbuck Site: A PaleoIndian Bison Kill, *Memoirs of the Society for American Archeology* 26, Washington, D.C.

Winship, George Park

1896 The Coronado Expedition, 1540–1542. *14th Annual Report,* part 1, Bureau of American Ethnology, Washington, D.C.

Winters, Howard D.

1969 The Riverton Culture: A Second Millenium Occupation in the Central Wabash Valley. *Reports on Investigations* 13, Illinois State Museum and Illinois Archaeological Survey, Springfield.

Wright, Muriel H.

1951 *A Guide to the Indian Tribes of Oklahoma.* Norman: University of Oklahoma Press.

Wyckoff, Don G.

1964 The Cultural Sequence at the Packard Site. *Archeological Site Report* 2, Oklahoma River Basin Survey Project, University of Oklahoma Research Institute, Norman.

1967 The E. Johnson Site and Prehistory in Southeast Oklahoma. *Archeological Site Report* 6, Oklahoma River Basin Survey and University of Oklahoma Research Institute, Norman.

1968 The Bell and Gregory Sites: Archaeological Chronicles of Prehistory in the Pine Creek Reservoir Area, Southeast Oklahoma. *Archaeological Site Report* 11, Oklahoma River Basin Survey, University of Oklahoma Research Institute, Norman.

1970 *The Horton Site Revisited: 1967 Excavations at Sq-11, Sequoyah County.* Oklahoma Archeological Survey, Studies in Oklahoma's Past 1.

1971 *The Caddoan Cultural Area: An Archeological Perspective.* Oklahoma Archeological Survey, Norman.

Wyckoff, Don G., and Robert L. Brooks

1983 *Oklahoma Archeology: A 1981 Perspective.* Oklahoma Archeological Survey, Archeological Resource Survey Report 16.

Wyckoff, Don G., and Lyonel Talor

1971 The Pumpkin Creek Site: An Early Archaic Camp on the Southern Plains Border. *Plains Anthropologist* (1971):16–51.

Index